D0574998

STANLEY REED

# ORIENTAL RUGS AND CARPETS

OCTOPUS BOOKS

# Acknowledgements

The author and publishers would like to express their grateful thanks to Messrs Perez (London) Ltd, who supplied all the illustrations for this book, with the exceptions of those in the following list, which were kindly provided by the institutions or individuals mentioned:

5, Hermitage Museum, Leningrad; 14, Mrs P. G. Turkhan; 37, Leo Vala; 39, 40, National Gallery, London; 65, Musée des Arts Décoratifs, Paris; 102, Worshipful Company of Girdlers; 111, 112, Carpet Export Syndicate.

Figure 2 was photographed by John Freeman and Co. Ltd (by courtesy of the Victoria and Albert Museum); figure 61 was specially photographed by Derrick Wittey (by courtesy of Perez Ltd.)

This edition first published 1972 by
OCTOPUS BOOKS LIMITED
59 Grosvenor Street, London W.1

ISBN 7064 0040 2

© 1967 by George Weidenfeld and Nicolson Ltd

PRODUCED BY MANDARIN PUBLISHERS LIMITED AND PRINTED IN HONG KONG

*Preceding page*
Kirman rug: 6 ft 10 ins × 4 ft 2 ins

# Contents

# HISTORY OF THE CRAFT

1 Silk Hereké of the early nineteenth century. Made in the Sultan's own factory. Warps, wefts and pile of finely spun silk – 1000 knots to the square inch

THE THEORIES AND GUESSES advanced by writers on the origins of the knotted pile rug are varied indeed, with no real evidence to support them, but in 1952 a remarkable book was published in Russian – *Finds in the Gorny-Altai and the Scyths* by S. I. Rudenko. The book describes Rudenko's expeditions from 1924 onwards in Southern Siberia near the Outer Mongolian frontier known as Gorny-Altai. In this expedition of 1947-9, a burial mound was excavated in the Pazyryk valley, and sufficient evidence was found in the shape of a knotted pile rug to establish that the art of knotting had already been mastered in the fifth century BC. This may not be the beginning of the story; other forms of textile weaving are older than this, and there is no reason to suppose that this was the first knotted example, but at least this appears to be a start [figure 5].

Preserved in perpetual ice, the rug is in a remarkable state of preservation. The piece is 6 ft 6 ins × 6 ft and of fairly fine knotting, and by virtue of its design has been attributed to Persia. The knot is, however, of the Turkish variety.

After this remarkable example, now in the Hermitage Museum in Leningrad, one must bridge nearly two thousand years to discover the next oldest pieces to have been preserved. These are in the Museum of Islamic Art, Istanbul, and date from the thirteenth century. For all practical purposes, therefore, the continuous history of rugs may be said to begin here, Asia Minor being at that time, if not the only producer, at least the largest one. There are, of course, many examples to be seen in museums and private collections of what may be termed tapestry or embroidery work, but the above dating is primarily for the knotted rug, and it can be assumed that most of the techniques employed to make even the Pazyryk example were almost exactly the same as are used today to make hand-knotted Oriental rugs. Most probably horizontal looms were used, as opposed to the upright

2 (*left*) The Ardebil carpet

5

3 A most unusual Ghiordes

4 (*opposite*) Embossed silk Kumkapu: 5 ft × 3 ft 9 ins. The inscriptions are carried out in gold and silver threads. The main field is of a rich bottle green, the spandrels ruby red, and the main border is pale gold

looms mainly used now, and of course the dyestuffs were obviously of vegetable or animal origin. Even today there are nomadic tribes and cottage industries still using the horizontal loom, hand-spun yarn and natural dyestuffs, so it can be said that virtually nothing has changed since those far off days — not even the designs. The tools used also remain unchanged.

The fourteenth, fifteenth and early sixteenth centuries have not left their mark in practical examples, but for painters they have provided a wonderful opportunity of depicting the type of pieces being imported from the East into Europe, and although the rugs themselves have long since disappeared, we are left with countless pictures by European artists of the day in which contemporary rugs were faithfully depicted. Even now, certain types of rug are referred to as 'Holbein rugs' because of the similarity of their design to those painted by that artist. In the main it was the Italian School which included rugs and carpets in their pictures, and this is understandable because it was through Venice that the European trade in Oriental rugs started. It is Holbein, however, who is remembered most in this connection.

The sixteenth century started what can now be regarded as the 'Golden Age' and the credit for such masterpieces goes to Persia. The best known example of this era is the Ardebil carpet in the Victoria and Albert Museum, London [figure 2], which has the Islamic date corresponding to the year AD 1539 or 1540 woven into one end, together with the name of the person responsible for the production of the piece — Maksoud of Kashan. This sets the standard and period for other carpets of similar grandeur, and from then onwards the periods are well defined.

The seventeenth and eighteenth centuries saw the emergence of the Turkish prayer rug of high quality and finish, but in Persia a gentle decline then started which persisted until the second half of the nineteenth century, when the commercial production of Persian goods, prompted and financed by European and local merchants, proved to be a turning point in their fortunes.

From the end of the eighteenth century, Turkish weaving, with two exceptions, entered a decline from which it has never really recovered. The exceptions are the Hereké weave and the Kumkapu [figures 1 and 4]. Herekés became very famous at the beginning of the nineteenth century. They were produced under the patronage of Sultans Medjid and Aziz. Most of the pieces were of European design with strong French influence. Some were wool, many in large room sizes;

others were made in very fine knotting, with silk pile. In both types, the technique of embossing – the shearing of the pile to different heights to throw certain designs into relief – was first executed. The silk rugs were presented to visiting royalty and other distinguished foreign visitors, including Queen Victoria and the Empress Eugénie of France. All genuine Herekés of this period are signed in one corner in Arabic calligraphy [figure 8].

Kumkapus were the successors of the Herekés. At the beginning of the twentieth century when production at Hereké ceased, Armenian weavers under the master weaver Zare-Aga of Istanbul began to create silk rugs with gold and silver threads [figure 4]. These were embossed, but this time did not have pile of different heights. Here the rugs were made partly of pile, which stood out in strong relief against a background of gold or silver warps and wefts without pile. The designs used were those of the great period of Persia; also there were intricate prayer rugs woven with verses from the *Koran* in the borders, carried out in *intaglio* with gold or silver warp threads which gave a subdued refulgence to the sacred words. These pieces were some of the finest ever woven and today command high prices in world markets.

So far, only Persia and Turkey have been discussed. The other weaving areas, apart from the Caucasus, contribute little to the overall historical picture, although individual items are, of course, preserved in museums and collections from all the known areas. The Caucasus, however, must rank in importance with Turkey, for it is possible that Turkey might not have reached the artistic heights which she did without Armenian influence.

Some of the early pieces now attributed to Turkey most probably came either from the Caucasus or from Armenian looms in Turkey, as it was only when Europeans and Americans took an interest in the techniques and history of Oriental rugs that geographical divisions were made. These have been handicapped over the centuries by the numerous political changes in the countries of the Middle East. It is significant that some of the rugs depicted in early European paintings were undoubtedly Caucasian in design and were not Turkish at all, although all Oriental carpets, at least in England in the sixteenth and seventeenth centuries, were described as 'Turkish' and even pieces made in England at that time were known as 'Turkish carpets of English making'. In an inventory of Bridget, Countess of Bedford, dated 1602, we find:

'Item one Turkey Carpett of Englishe makinge
Item two Wyndowe Turkey Carpettes of my owne
makinge the one of them being wrought with Roses
and Marygouldes.'

Included in an inventory of property belonging to Henry Howard, Earl of Northampton, dated 1614, is the following:

'Item a longe Turkie carpett of Englishe worke with the Earle of Northampton his armes, being 5 yeardes and 3 quarters longe.'

The market for export to Europe from the hinterland was Constantinople, and of course, even in Turkey itself, the refugees from the ill-fated country of Armenia took their culture with them and wove rugs, so in some respects in those early days it is not possible to make positive identification of certain pieces.

What of the twentieth century? Have rugs been produced which will stand the test of time? Now that we have passed through two thirds of the century some consideration may be given to the pieces produced in the first years. The Kumkapus have already been mentioned. In Turkey little else has been made worthy of note in this chapter. In Persia, certain pieces, especially from Tabriz and Kashan, are now at the 'semi-antique' stage, that is, mellowed enough for good furnishing, and still in good pile, giving promise for the future. One or two outstanding rugs have been made in Kashmir, but these are in the nature of technical accomplishment rather than works of art, with up to 2600 knots to the square inch.

Of course, during this century new techniques have been applied, not in the actual weaving, which is still done in the traditional manner, but in the preparatory processes such as spinning — yarns are now in the main machine-spun; dyeing — in most instances what may be called artificial dyestuffs as opposed to natural ones are now used; and chemical washing, which artificially mellows or even changes some harsh colours, imparting a lustrous silky sheen to a piece and giving what is regarded by many as a more luxurious finish than hitherto. In addition to these twentieth-century innovations, none of which assist in creating the treasures of the future, it must be borne in mind that, while designs have not changed to any great extent over the years, there can only be one original, and in most instances that original was made at least 200 years ago. Consequently the rugs of today, while they are probably commercially successful, can with few exceptions be regarded as no more than copies.

6 Konia rug: 5 ft × 3 ft 8 ins

7 Small antique carpet from the Kuba district

8 One version of the Hereké mark or signature, woven on all genuine pieces

12

# PRAYER RUGS

PROBABLY THE MOST FASCINATING ASPECT of rug lore to the collector is the prayer rug, or, to give it its Oriental name, the *Namazlyk*. It is proposed therefore to deal with this category as a whole, instead of discussing the various types separately in the chapters which are devoted to different geographical or political regions. Prayer rugs are made and used by all people who profess the Moslem faith, and as Islamic chronology starts with Mohammed's flight from Mecca to Medina in AD 622, which is known as the *Hegira*, it would be as well to describe the method of dating rugs before we proceed further.

Typical Arabic numerals used on rugs are:

١ ٢ ٣ ٤٣ ٥٥ ٦ ٧ ٨ ٩ .
1 2 3 4 5 6 7 8 9 0

As dated rugs show the Moslem year, which is a lunar year, it is necessary to make the following calculation in order to find the equivalent date in the Christian calendar:
1. divide the rug date (Moslem year) by thirty-three
2. deduct the result from the rug date
3. add 622 to the remainder.

Example: the Ardebil carpet in the Victoria and Albert Museum is dated AH 946. By using the above system we will arrive at the year AD 1539/1540. It should be added that the numerals woven on a rug run from left to right.

It is not known exactly when the practice of using knotted rugs to cover the 'unclean' ground for the purposes of prayer first started, but it could not have been before AD 622 and it is said that it was almost a hundred years after the *Hegira* that a niche or *mihrab* was built into mosques for the purpose of indicating the direction of Mecca, the Holy City. The arch design on a prayer rug certainly serves this purpose; but it cannot be supposed that this came later than the architectural feature because, according to Islamic custom,

9 Basra Ghiordes prayer rug: 5 ft 6 ins × 4 ft 3 ins

13

all places are equal, and prayer may take place wherever one finds oneself at the appropriate time. Consequently the rug may have preceded the mosque *mihrab*. There are, however, no surviving examples to point to from those early days. The earliest record yet known of the *mihrab* design is on a Persian miniature in the Bibliothèque Nationale in Paris, dated 1436.

Some museums label a few of their early pieces as late sixteenth or early seventeenth century, and it is safe to assume that the latter dating is the more correct one. The largest producer was Asia Minor, and these are a quite distinct type, very different from those of other areas. Named after towns or villages, the prayer rugs of Asia Minor were the product of both nomadic and cottage industries, whereas the Persian ones were made under factory conditions, usually under Royal patronage, all of which is evident in their intricate and well drawn designs. Again, unlike the Persian rugs, those from Asia Minor closely followed the religious rules of the particular Islamic sect to which the inhabitants belong — the Sunnites.

No representation of human faces or animals will be found on the rugs produced by adherents to the Sunnite law. In contrast, the Persian product will occasionally show animals, since the Shiite creed which they follow is not so particular in that respect. The Caucasus produced angular designs in keeping with all its products, many of which were dated, so helping to define periods of manufacture. Here again animal designs are found occasionally. The other area producing prayer rugs was Turkestan which, for this purpose, must include the Beloutch and Afghan rugs. No animal or human figures will be found in these rugs, which are the most easily identifiable with their deep blood red to brown ground colour, mostly associated with Bokhara rugs and the sombre black and deep purple of the Beloutch weavings.

The Golden Age for all prayer rugs lasted from the beginning of the seventeenth century until the end of the eighteenth. Although many rugs of this period are still in existence, the number to be found today is a very small percentage of those actually produced during those two centuries. This is quite understandable when we realize that of all knotted pile rugs it was the prayer rug which was made for the most practical use. Other types of rug were, of course, made for floor coverings, but many were also made for other uses, such as for covering divans, or for wall hangings, and many of the fine floor carpets were only used on special occ-

10 Konia prayer rug: 5 ft 6 ins × 4 ft 2 ins. Note the three *ibriks* or water pitchers in the central column

11 Saph, or communal prayer carpet from Eastern Turkestan. Marketed in Samarkand: 13 ft 4 ins × 3 ft 7ins

asions, or for use in rooms with little traffic. The prayer rug, however, was used by its devout Moslem owner five times a day, it was laid on any surface available at the appointed hour, knelt on, in the centre of the field, which was often of plain weave, and after prayer, was rolled up and carried around until the next time. Consequently, prayer rugs received more wear, particularly in one area of the rug, than any other type, and it is fortunate that so many have been preserved to the present day, even though most of them are rather thin in the centre.

Identification of prayer rugs is not difficult so far as the main divisions of area are concerned. Turkoman colours are based on the deep red or brown common to that area; Persian prayer rugs are curvilinear, with rounded *mihrabs*, many flowers, often with borders or spandrels filled with verses from the *Koran*, or the work of the many poets of the country; Caucasians are completely angular, as is all carpet design from this area; the remainder are Turkish, or, to give them the name currently applied to rugs from Asia Minor which defy further definition − Anatolian.

In general, more positive identification can be made from the shape of the *mihrab*, but with the passing of time these changed, and there are pitfalls to be avoided in using this method. The main shapes used, and the areas from which

they come, are shown here in illustrations, but this must not be taken to mean that all rugs of each type must have the *mihrab* depicted.

Also shown are some of the motifs used, particularly in the Turkish and Caucasian examples, such as the *ibrik* or water pitcher, the comb, the lamp, and the tulip, which is only seen in Ladik rugs.

The *ibrik* is represented because a Moslem must wash before praying. In desert regions, however, water may be very scarce. Sand or a white stone may be used to go through the actions of washing, or in the absence of these substitutes the owner of the rug may symbolically wash by rubbing his hands on the *ibrik* and then going through the motions of washing [figure 10].

The comb motif has been said to represent a weaver's comb, which is used in rug-making to beat a row of pile knots to the desired density; another suggestion is that it symbolizes the rays of the sun; but in a prayer rug the most likely explanation is that it is there to remind the worshipper that he must comb his beard before praying.

The lamp is said to represent the Mosque lamp, whilst the tulip motif of the Ladik is reminiscent of the Lale Devry, or tulip period, during the reign of Ahmed III (1703-30). Also influenced by this era were the famous Broussa velvets

17

12 Ghiordes prayer rug of the seventeenth century: 6 ft 5 ins × 4 ft 9 ins

and Iznik pottery, both of which made a special feature of tulips in their designs. The following paragraphs give the names of the most prominent types of prayer rug, together with details of interest connected with them.

## ASIA MINOR

*Ghiordes* This is an extremely ancient city from which came some of the finest examples of prayer rugs ever made [figure 12]. It was a late starter, not opening production until the beginning of the seventeenth century, but such is the fame of this make of rug that in the western world the name Ghiordes is used to describe the Turkish knot, wherever it is used. Could there in fact be some connection between the name applied to this knot and the 'Gordian' knot of ancient times? It is unlikely, but the fact remains that the city of Gordium appears to have been associated with a knot ever since the days of Alexander the Great. Gordium was the ancient capital of Phrygia and was named after King Gordius, father of King Midas (of the asses' ears) The story has it that an oracle told the populace that a waggon would bring a king who would restore peace to their land. Gordius appeared in his chariot and was immediately proclaimed king. Dedicating his chariot to Jupiter (or Zeus) he tied the pole to the yoke with a peculiar knot. Another oracle thereupon declared that whoever could untie the knot would eventually reign over Asia. Alexander severed the knot with his sword, and the kingdom went to him.

Rugs and carpets other than the prayer version were made in Ghiordes and other places in the Islamic world, but as this chapter is concerned only with *namazlyks*, other types will be dealt with separately under their respective chapter headings. One exception must, however, be mentioned here and that is the double prayer rug, with a kind of *mihrab* at each end.

It is not suggested that these rugs were used exclusively for the purposes of prayer, but no doubt they could be used in this manner. The type referred to is known as Kiz-Ghiordes [figure 13]. The word *Kiz* means 'maiden', and rugs of this type were made from the end of the eighteenth century by young girls either in harems or as part of a girl's dowry on marriage or as a means of displaying her skill as a weaver to her prospective bridegroom. Very finely woven, these pieces come in a rather smaller size than that of the conventional prayer rug.

The best known and most sought after type of Ghiordes prayer rug is the Basra, made from the beginning as we

13 Kiz-Ghiordes rug: 6 ft × 4 ft 6 ins

14 An extremely rare example of a Ladik prayer rug, because of its natural colour ground. Another interesting and rare feature is the inscription at the foot of the rug

know it (say the beginning of the seventeenth century) until the middle of the eighteenth century. It has been suggested that this name derives from the district of that name, now in Iraq, where possession of such pieces became the fashion amongst high-ranking Moslems. Much more positive evidence is required to confirm such a belief, but it does sound at least feasible. A peculiarity of the Basra weave is that when seen from the back, the weft shoots appear to be of short length, and are tied to each other in such a way that there is a zig-zag line up the length of the piece.

*Konia* This, the capital city of the Seljuki Turks, the ancient city of Iconium, is one of the several centres in Turkey, where the famous Whirling Dervishes perform their practices and is credited with the earliest preserved examples of rugs dating from the thirteenth century. These examples are not designed as prayer rugs as we know them, although they were found in the Mosque of Ala-ad-Din in Konia. They are now in the Museum of Islamic Art, Istanbul. Other pieces of the same period were found in the Eshrefiglu Mosque at Beyshehir, some distance away from Konia, but all these have been grouped together under the general title of Konia, even though they may not have been made there.

The Konia rugs in the various collections throughout the world stem from the sixteenth and seventeenth centuries, after which, in common with all other forms of Turkish art, a decline set in from which the craft has never recovered.

*Oushak* Although a great centre for the making of rugs and carpets in the sixteenth and seventeenth centuries, this town is more widely known for its large pieces than for in-

15 Oushak Saph or communal prayer carpet: 16 ft 8 ins × 12 ft 4 ins. This piece originally had seven compartments in each row. It would appear that it was severely damaged at the left hand side, necessitating the removal of the border and one compartment from each row. The photograph clearly shows the almost completely re-woven new border. The work was beautifully executed, and it could have been done any time between 100 and 150 years ago

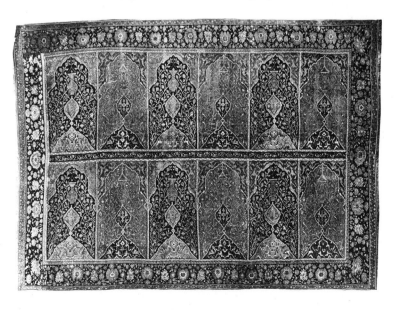

19

16 Mezarli Koula or Tomb rug: 6 ft × 4 ft 2 ins

dividual prayer rugs. Many of the carpets of large size were made specially for Mosque use, and although most of them were of simple designs many Saphs, or communal prayer carpets, were made, with numerous *mihrabs* [figure 15]. The Oushak designs often bear some signs of Persian influence, and it is supposed that many of the craftsmen were indeed Persian.

*Ladik* The prayer rugs from this town, the ancient city of Laodicea, reached the peak of weaving excellence at the end of the seventeenth century and beginning of the eighteenth. Easily recognizable, early Ladiks are invariably constructed with a kind of triple *mihrab*, but the distinguishing feature is the row of tulips above the *mihrab*. No rug other than a prayer rug has yet been classed as Ladik, which seems to suggest that the production was primarily of this type [figure 20].

*Koula* Not very far from Ghiordes lies this small city where a disinctive type of prayer rug was made from the seventeenth century until the general decline of the craft in Turkey.

Something akin to the Ghiordes in weave, Koulas generally seem to our eyes to be lacking in lively colour, particularly the type known as Mezarli or tomb rug, supposedly used at funerals, which is distinctive because the centre field is filled with designs bearing a resemblance to cypress trees [figure 16]. The normal early Koula prayer rug is prefixed Kafali and although there are further divisions — Direkli, Komurju and Sinekli — it is only the former that commands our attention for the purposes of this book.

*Transylvanian, or Siebenbürger* There is some doubt as to where this particular type of rug was produced, but it is generally accepted that it was in the district of Oushak. Sometimes with one prayer niche, but mainly seen with a *mihrab* at each end, these rugs were found in profusion in the churches of Transylvania (now part of Roumania) [figures 18 and 20]. Various theories have been advanced as to why these particular rugs should have been discovered in such quantities in this area, although they were not confined exclusively to it.

A feasible solution appears to be that they were gifts, given as a gesture of friendship or for propaganda purposes by the Military Governor of the Transylvanian district after the Balkan invasion by the Turks.

Another tenable theory that has been advanced is that at the time when the Ottoman Empire had spread its tentacles

17 Silk Tabriz rug: 6 ft × 4 ft 2 ins

18 Transylvanian rug of typical design:
5 ft 3 ins × 3 ft 11 ins

to cover the whole of South-Eastern Europe, for some inexplicable reason the Turkish authorities allowed the people of what was then Transylvania to continue to follow their Christian religion. The people of this area were great traders, and often, with the permission of the authorities, made trading journeys into Asia Minor. These journeys were fraught with innumerable hazards, not only of weather and inhospitable country, but also because of bandits and bands of marauding soldiers. Those fortunate travellers who safely ran the gauntlet both ways formed the habit of showing their gratitude to God for their preservation by making a present of the most valuable object they had brought back from their expedition, and this frequently took the form of a rug. So many of these rugs were found in the churches of Transylvania that the rug trade used that name to classify them.

It is said that the altar of the Black Church in Brasov was covered with rugs. It is estimated that about two thousand

19 Melas prayer rug: 5 ft 8 ins × 4 ft

20 (*right*) Transylvanian rug of unusual design: 5 ft 10 ins × 4 ft 1 in

rugs were distributed. At the end of the nineteenth century some of these rugs found their way on to the market from Transylvania, and it was at this point that investigation showed that they were definitely of Anatolian origin. When found today, Transylvanian rugs are normally in extremely good condition, due, no doubt, to the fact they were never put to practical use but were used only to cover the altars of the churches.

*Melas* Prayer rugs have been made for centuries in the area of this small town in South-West Anatolia [figure 19]. It has been suggested that the so-called Transylvanian rugs

21 Mudjur prayer rug: 4 ft 10 ins × 3 ft 3 ins

22 (*right*) Shirvan prayer rug: 4 ft 10 ins × 3 ft 6 ins

originated here, but this has never been substantiated. As with the Ladik rugs, Melas are almost invariably found with prayer design.

*Megri*　Not far south of Melas, on the coast opposite the island of Rhodes, is the little town of Megri. Prayer rugs from this area are often known as 'Rhodes' rugs, but there is no evidence to suppose that any were ever made on the island. Mainly eighteenth and nineteenth century examples are to be found. One particular type, while being of the normal prayer rug size, has two *mihrabs*, side by side, each obviously very narrow. This type is called the 'Brothers rug',

23

23 Shirvan runner: 8 ft 7 ins × 3 ft 9 ins

24 Silk Broussa prayer rug: 6 ft 4 ins × 4 ft 1in

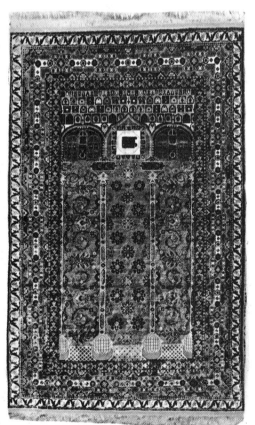

presumably because it could be used by two persons — but they must have been very thin if they were able to use the rug at the same time!

*Broussa*  From this city — famous for its velvets — come brightly coloured, but finely woven silk prayer rugs [figure 24]. They appear to be a product of the nineteenth and twentieth centuries, with an eye for export markets, but they are none the less very beautiful.

There are other names associated with the prayer rugs of Anatolia, but as none has contributed to the development or knowledge of the craft only small mention need be made of them here to complete the picture as far as Turkey is concerned. The Yuruk rugs were produced by a tribe inhabiting the eastern part of Anatolia. Mudjur and Kirshehir (those from the latter also being known as 'Sultan' rugs), together with the twentieth century Panderma, account for practically all the better known names.

It is felt that any further breaking down may become confusing, and in fact some of the other names encountered are merely traders' definitions denoting qualities in the bazaars of Istanbul.

## THE CAUCASUS

Prayer rugs from this area — the cross-roads of the world — are easily identified, at least as far as the late eighteenth century and the nineteenth are concerned. Always geometrical, with no curves whatsoever, somewhat coarse in

24

weave, and with all the little unexpected extras in their designs, such as combs, hands, etc., they cannot be mistaken for anything else but Caucasian. Very few names need be recounted to distinguish the various types. The first to come to mind is the Shirvan [figures 22 and 31], from the southeast of the area, often confused with the Daghestan [figures 29 and 30], made further north. In order to confuse the situation even further, Daghestans are often called Derbend, from the city of that name. The only other name needing to be mentioned here is the Kazak — the rug with the long glossy pile. Elsewhere in this book will be found a more detailed review of Caucasian rugs, the above mentioned being the main varieties made in prayer style.

## PERSIA

Considering that Persia is probably the cradle of the craft, and of Moslem inclination, very few prayer rugs have been handed down from the past. Those which have survived, most of which are now in museums, are the products of the Golden Age court manufacture. Finely woven, and of extremely good draughtsmanship, these pieces, as much as the court carpets of the period, convey an artistry which has never been surpassed in the textile field. No particular weaving centre has been attributed to them, the assumption being that as the court moved from place to place, so the ancilliary services went too, including the rug factories. With the decline in Persian art after the seventeenth century, nothing is found until the beginning of the nineteenth, when prayer rugs appear to have been made in silk as well as wool in Tabriz [figure 27], Heriz, Kashan, and

25 Megri (or 'Rhodes') prayer rug: 6 ft 4 ins × 3 ft 6 ins. Note the two *mihrabs*

26 Kazak: 9 ft 7 ins × 3 ft 10 ins

27 Tabriz prayer rug of the nineteenth century: 5 ft 7 ins × 4 ft 2 ins

28 (*right*) Kirman prayer rug: 6 ft 8 ins × 4 ft 6 ins

Kirman [figure 28]. The designs of these later pieces do not however copy the masterpieces of the sixteenth and seventeenth centuries. New ground was broken in design, as can clearly be seen from the illustrations. It was left to the Armenian weavers of Istanbul at the beginning of the twentieth century to copy designs of the earlier period, in the so-called Kumkapu weave. That they copied faithfully there is no doubt, and to make the product look even more

29 Daghestan prayer rug: 5 ft 6 ins × 3 ft 7 ins

30 Daghestan prayer rug: 4 ft 9 ins × 3 ft 4 ins

luxurious they used gold and silver threads in parts of the warp and weft, creating an embossed effect, and making the rug shine in the sun like a jewel.

## TURKESTAN

This area, now Russian, but also for the purpose of this book encompassing the north-eastern regions of Persia and Afghanistan, can roughly be divided into two parts — western and eastern. The eastern section can conveniently be based on Samarkand, where there is a rug market dealing with the more Chinese influenced products of Khotan, 27

Kashgar and Yarkand. Prayer rugs as we have defined them
are not found in this part of the world, the only type finding
its way onto the market being the Saph, or communal prayer
carpet, which was usually called Samarkand, and was often
made of silk.

32 Hatchli Bokhara prayer rug

33 Daghestan: 5 ft 1 in × 4 ft 4 ins

The western portion, however, together with North-East Persia and Afghanistan, is responsible for the numerous varieties of the so-called Bokhara weave [figure 36]. The whole of the region is settled by various tribes, and it is their names that are given to many of the different types to

29

35 A fine prayer rug of the Sefavi period. It
is attributed to Isfahan, but it is by no means
certain that it was made there. The inscriptions are verses from the *Koran*.

be found. In the majority of instances the prayer rugs are
not always easy to define, as there may only be a very small
*mihrab*, hardly distinguishing the fact of its use. One of the
types most commonly incorporating the *mihrab* — although
not seen very often — is the Hatchli, which has the main
field divided into four parts in the form of a cross. These are
usually squarer than the rugs from other countries, and the
non-prayer version is also used as a door flap to a tent. A
more conventional prayer rug is attributed to Beshir, whilst
the other main type in this district is called the Beloutch —
not from Beloutchistan, as is sometimes popularly supposed,
but made by the wandering Beloutchi tribes from the North-
East of Persia and Afghanistan [figure 34].

36 Yamout Bokhara prayer rug

37 (*left*) Silk Tabriz rug from the middle of the nineteenth century containing the crown and the Persian emblem. This piece was most probably made for the use of one of the Qajar Shahs

38 Silk Tabriz rug: 5 ft 1 in × 4 ft 2 ins

IT IS SURPRISING how many antique Turkish pieces are still about, and in good condition, too. This is fortunate because today production is probably at its lowest ebb for centuries, both in quantity and quality. In its heyday, Turkey must have been a tremendous producer. Although very little is preserved from the early days (and even this is not altogether authenticated) Marco Polo described the carpets of Asia Minor as 'the best and handsomest carpets in the

39 (*left*) Detail from *Somerset House Conference* (1604), attributed to M. Gheraedts II

world'. That it was indeed the Turkish rug (or Caucasian, but called Turkish) which first penetrated into Europe there can be no doubt, as witness the numerous paintings by fourteenth- to sixteenth-century artists showing rugs either as floor coverings or table covers. It was inevitable that the Italian painters should be the most prolific portrayers of the rug, because it was through Venice that the European trade started, not only in carpets but in all other artistic products from the East. It is, however, the name of Holbein the Younger which lives on in rug lore, to describe the type of design frequently used by that artist. The term 'Holbein Oushak' describes any Oushak rug with a so-called 'Holbein' design, although some of the designs attributed to him were painted by other artists [figures 42 and 44].

Spain also imported rugs from Turkey at a very early stage, probably through her Moorish connections. The Spaniards not only imported them but started to weave for themselves, the earliest surviving examples being very Turkish in character. These date from the fifteenth century. What kind of carpets Queen Eleanor of Castile took to England in the thirteenth century can only be conjectured. Most probably they were Turkish, or possibly Spanish.

Although the earliest pieces attributed to Turkey were very angular in design, by the sixteenth century a considerable element of curvilinear draughtsmanship appeared, and rounded forms with central medallion designs can be

40 Detail from Holbein's *The Ambassadors* (1533)

35

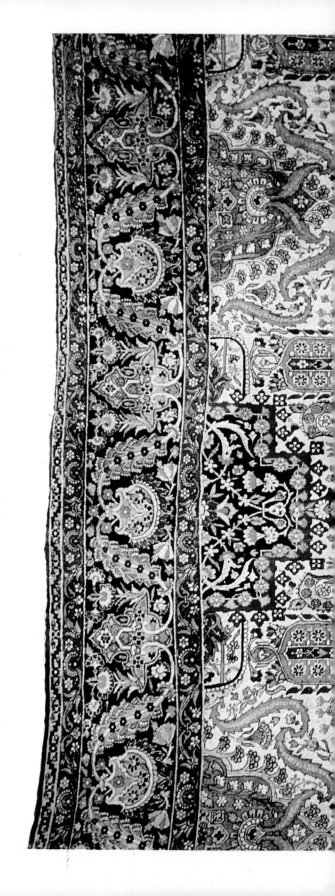

41 Centre detail of a Kirman carpet: 16 ft × 11 ft 3 ins

42 Oushak rug: 8 ft 6 ins × 5 ft. 4 ins. Often termed 'Holbein', but not known to have been painted by this artist. Also more correctly called 'Lotto' after the Italian painter Lorenzo Lotto (1480–1556)

43 Oushak rug: 9 ft 5 ins × 5 ft 8 ins. Late seventeenth century

found in the products of Oushak. Undoubtedly this was due to the importation of Persian weavers and other workers into Turkey, especially after the military successes of the Turks in Persia during the first half of the century. Oushak appears to have been the centre of the craft, and some of the designs produced in those days are classified into categories of Oushak. For instance, there is the Holbein Oushak, the Star, the Bird and the Medallion Oushaks [figure 43].

More in keeping with what we regard as Persian design and influence are the carpets now referred to as of Turkish court manufacture. These were almost certainly made by Persian craftsmen. Where they were made is not known, but the claims of Oushak are very strong.

It is known that the Star Oushak carpet arrived in England in the sixteenth century, for there are four carpets in the possession of the Duke of Buccleuch which were made in England to the order of his ancestor Sir Edward Montagu (1532-1602) and three of which are of typical Star Oushak design. Many authorities claim that these pieces are of actual Turkish manufacture, but the foundation threads of hemp or flax (not used in the Oriental product) and the fact that they have initials inconspicuously woven into various parts of the borders and field (for example, E.B. and A.N. each occur in two carpets), together with the dates 1584 and 1585 on two pieces, leave little doubt that this series was made in England. It is fairly certain, too, that they were copied from Turkish originals, with some variation in the borders to accommodate the arms of Sir Edward Montagu on each side and at the ends.

One other type of Oushak carpet must not be left out, although this brings us into the last century. The Yaprak design carpet, beloved of Victorian households and hotels, and variously called the Red and Blue Turkey, or just the Turkey carpet, was a commercial venture of the late nineteenth century, and indeed continued well into the twentieth. Thick piled, with a silky appearance, these carpets not only looked solid and trustworthy, events have shown that they really were solid and hard-wearing. Unfortunately they were copied profusely in inferior makes, but the genuine Yaprak Oushak was a good commercial proposition, and a fine trade with England existed at the turn of the century.

Historically, Asia Minor made a big contribution to the rug world, but apart from the prayer rugs and the Oushak weaves nothing much remains, until the nineteenth century when the Hereké Court woven carpet made its appearance. Later in the century, when commercial ventures saw the possibilities of supplying Europe and America in bulk with standard sizes and designs, made specially to furnish rooms in these continents, the town of Izmir, or Smyrna, became important as a distributing centre. Carpets and rugs were supplied in large quantities to the furnishing houses of the west, and it is from here that the Yapraks were shipped, along with carpets with Europeanized designs — not the true French style, but specially designed for the European market in soft pastel shades. These were called Sparta, and were made in various districts not far away from Smyrna (notably Isparta, from where the carpet takes its name). Various qualities were made, and they became very popular, particularly in England. Later, at the end of the nineteenth century, a Greek version, made near Athens, was marketed.

The other contribution to the craft from Turkey is of course the Kumkapu, but apart from these few innovations, Turkey must rest on its sixteenth- to early eighteenth-century laurels in the world of the rug.

44 So-called 'Holbein' Oushak rug

45 Detail of an antique Tabriz carpet: 22 ft
× 13 ft (mid-nineteenth century). An unusual feature of this piece is the prominence
of the birds in the field

# THE CAUCASUS

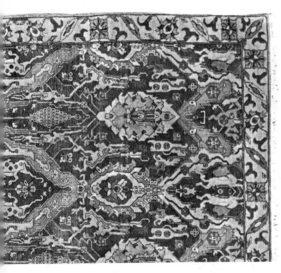

46 Armenian 'dragon' rug of the Caucasus

THE DEALER has a difficult task nowadays in buying Caucasian rugs from Russia. In order to obtain a few good old pieces, he has to take a substantial quantity of modern rugs. He can easily sell the old ones, but he cannot increase his prices on these sufficiently to be able to cover the cost of the whole parcel, because by and large the new goods cannot be considered attractive when seen with the old. No amount of treatment will give the new product anything like the beauty of the old one. This of course is true of many things, but it appears more noticeable in the rugs of the Caucasus. This is probably because the name of the Caucasus to the western mind conjures up visions of a hard-living, semi-nomadic people, making rugs as tough as can be, and the modern product bears no resemblance to this ideal.

The weaving area is in the south, and what is now the Soviet Republic of Armenia has contributed much to the craft, wherever it is practised, but particularly in Asia Minor.

Historically speaking, it cannot be doubted that some of the early rugs and carpets which found their way into Europe labelled 'Turkish' were made either in Armenia or by Armenian weavers in Turkey. In spite of the centuries of turmoil experienced by their ill-fated country, for some reason the Armenians never appear to have debased their culture, and even today the Republic gives much to the cultural life of the Soviet Union, particularly in the fields of music and handcrafts.

When, in the nineteenth century, the western world started to study the subject of Oriental rugs, and endeavoured to identify them by town, district or tribe, the divisions which we use today were applied.

By far the most important group of historic carpets is the type known as the Armenian Dragon rug, of the fifteenth and sixteenth centuries [figure 46]. These rugs are invari-

47 (*right*) Seichur rug: 5 ft 8 ins × 3 ft 8 ins

48 (*above*) Shirvan rug: 5 ft 6 ins × 4 ft 4 ins. Note the 'wineglass' border, typical of this type of rug

49 (*above*) Cabistan: 9 ft 10 ins × 4 ft 10 ins
50 (*left*) Chichi rug

ably long and narrow, with narrow borders; it is often difficult to see dragons in the field design, but it is true to say that in some examples, with a little bit of artistic licence, forms can be seen that could conceivably be stylized dragons and other animals in combat, or at least face to face. Most of the good examples are to be seen in museums, particularly on the continent of Europe and in the United States of America. As for where they were made, nobody knows, but the popular attribution is the Kuba district, which sounds feasible enough. Kuba remained an important centre for the manufacture of rugs and carpets, but in later pieces some confusion is found in the correct names to be used for pieces from this area. Shirvan rugs [figure 48] also come from this part of the Caucasus, which is, in fact, in the province of Shirvan, but by and large Shirvan is the name given to scatter rug sizes, and Kuba to the larger carpet sizes.

51 (*left*) So-called 'vase' carpet
of the sixteenth or seventeenth
century. Attributed to Isfahan,
in the absence of any better
evidence

52 (*right*) A very fine Kirman
rug: 7 ft 4 ins × 4 ft 7 ins

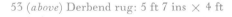
53 (*above*) Derbend rug: 5 ft 7 ins × 4 ft

54 (*above right*) An unusual Baku (Hile) rug: 5 ft 7 ins × 3 ft 10 ins

In between there is the rug about 10′ × 5′ which is usually known as a Cabistan [figure 49]. Here more confusion arises – the word *Kiaba* refers in the Caucasus to this size, therefore the term 'Kiaba-Shirvan' may be used for it. However, the word *Cabistan* could be a corruption of *Kubistan*, which denotes carpets from Kuba. Whatever the explanation, the name Cabistan is often used in the trade to describe a Shirvan of about 10′ × 5′. Chichi rugs also come from the Shirvan area; they are easily identified by their main border treatment [figure 50].

To the north of Kuba lies the area of Daghestan. From here come the Daghestans [figure 30], the Derbends [figure 53] from the capital of the province, and the Seichurs from the village of that name [figure 47]. South of Kuba is

55 (*above*) Baku (Hile) rug: 5 ft 10 ins × 2 ft 10 ins

56 (*above right*) Verne pileless rug: 13 ft 1 in × 5 ft 4 ins

57 (*right*) Genje rug: 4 ft 9 ins × 3 ft 3 ins

58 Carabagh: 12 ft 1 in × 4 ft 9 ins. Dated
1809

the main Shirvan area, and the city of Baku, one of the main
oil-producing cities in Russia. The rugs of Baku are not
made in the city but in the small village of Hile just outside,
and they are usually classified as Baku (Hile) rugs [figures
54 and 55]. Soumac is also near here, the home of the flat
woven Kelim type pieces, but with a peculiar weave all of its
own.

Almost in the centre of the Caucasus, nearly half way between the Caspian Sea and the Black Sea, is the Carabagh
area. For some obscure reason, in the nineteenth century
this part of the world turned out rugs and runners completely out of context for Caucasian pieces. These depicted
European designs but with the feeling of the East in them,
some with dogs as designs, but all showing that peculiar
colour combination associated with Carabaghs, black and a
shade which could be described as deep rose tending towards
wine [figure 58]. Also from this part of the country are to
be found Genje rugs, colourful, cheerful, and completely
Caucasian [figure 57].

Farther west towards the Black Sea is the country of the
Kazaks, well-known to European and American markets [fig-
ure 26]. There are three types of flat woven (pileless) rugs
or *Kelims*, made in the Caucasus, the best known being the
Soumac, which was mentioned previously. These are unlike
flat woven fabrics from other parts of the world in that the
woollen threads forming the pattern on the face of the rug
are left hanging loose on the back, in the same manner as in

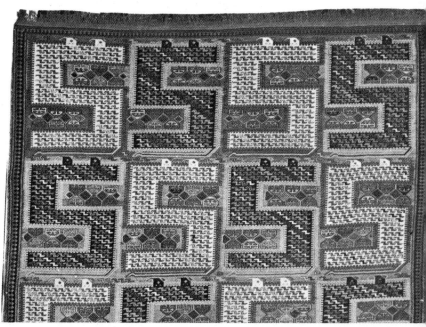

59 Sile pileless rug: 8 ft 10 ins × 7 ft 7 ins

60 Kirman rug: 6 ft 10 ins × 4 ft 2 ins

a European tapestry. This gives a more luxurious tread of course, but the rugs are not reversible. The other types are known as the Sile and the Verne, but in most instances the name Soumac serves for all. There are, however, distinguishing features; the Sile is woven on rather narrow looms, necessitating the sewing together of two widths to make a normal sized rug, and their designs consist of large 'S'-shaped figures [figure 59]. The Verne is made in designs of squares alone, each containing lozenge-shaped figures, something akin to a Persian Bakhtiari garden design [figure 56]. As with all Caucasian weaving there is a complete absence of rounded forms.

49

61 Fragment of the Ardebil carpet, now in the possession of Messrs Perez, London

PERSIA APPEARS to be the country where it all started. The Pazyryk example, the earliest piece of knotted weaving yet discovered, has all the attributes of Persian weave, apart from the knotting, which is Turkish. The so-called 'Garden Carpet' or 'Spring of Chosroes' at Ctesiphon, also Persian, described in the first written record in which a carpet is mentioned, must have been one of the most remarkable pieces ever woven. It is hardly possible that this carpet was knotted, and one must conclude that it was made in some form of tapestry or Kelim weave. The size was enormous, sixty cubits square, which makes it about 90 ft × 90 ft. (A cubit is the length of the forearm from the elbow to the end of the middle finger, approximately 18 ins.)

According to early accounts this magnificent sumptuary carpet was woven of the finest silk, the pattern being in the form of a garden in which the gravel paths were represented by gold thread, the streams by silver thread, and the lawns by masses of emeralds sewn to the background. Trees and bushes were depicted with gold and silver thread and precious stones of different colours were used to form the flowers. The purpose of this fabulously expensive carpet was to cover the floor of the palace at Ctesiphon during the winter months so that the king might still enjoy his spring garden, hence the name 'Spring of Chosroes'. After the fall of the Persian Empire to the Arab invaders, the conquerors, when dividing the spoils, came to the not unreasonable conclusion that such a prize was too much to fall to the lot of one person and it was therefore cut in pieces and apportioned among the leaders. It has been reported that several of the pieces later found their way into the bazaars of Baghdad. *Sic transit gloria.*

From this date of defeat until the beginning of the Golden Age in the first half of the sixteenth century, we know very little of the art of rug weaving, apart from occasional references in writings concerning the extravagances of cer-

62 (*left*) The Trinitarias carpet

63 Woven during the reign of Shah Sulayman (1667–1697) and therefore of the Sefavi dynasty. Attributed to Isfahan. The inscriptions in the main border, though in an archaic style, and with one of the verses in 'mirror image' are nevertheless finely written. They read as follows:

The precious royal carpet which lies on the ground boasts that his rank and splendour are greater than all things in the firmament. He has fallen under the feet of the King, and is very happy because he is surrounded by many beautiful women.

Why should not this sublime seat be the companion of Zephyr when he has for his merits a face under the feet of such a king Sulayman?

On the sublime seat resides a king whose conquests and victories have been thanks to the grace of God innumerable.

The heavens have cast down their golden light to illuminate the darkness in which the just King dwells.

The justice of the monarch who rules the kingdom is a hundred times greater than that of Solomon.

tain rulers of the period. Then come the first hundred years or so of the Sefavi dynasty when the finest carpets ever seen were made. The surviving pieces from this period are well catalogued, and many of them can be seen in the Victoria and Albert Museum, London, the Museum for Art and Industry, Vienna, the Museo Poldi Pezzoli in Milan, or the Metropolitan Museum of Art, New York, to name but a few.

Detailed descriptions of these pieces have been published many times, and need not be recounted here, but there is one carpet from this period which seems to warrant further mention, for, to the author's knowledge, it has not been recorded in any book until now. It is called the 'Trinitarias' carpet [figure 62], so named from the Convent of the Trinitarias Del Calzas of the Calle Lope de Vega, Madrid (the burial place of Cervantes) where it had lain for more than 300 years, being only brought out and used on special feast days. The earliest record of the carpet in the convent's archives is 1699, but it is reputed to have been given to the Del Calzas nuns by Philip IV of Spain when the Trinitarias Convent was founded in Madrid at the beginning of the seventeenth century. It was never seen by the public until 1928, when it was removed from the convent and exhibited at the Seville World Fair. Shortly afterwards it was sold to the Spanish Art Gallery in London, after opposition from the Royal Academy of History, Madrid, which wished the Spanish nation to purchase it to prevent it from leaving the country. In fact the opposition to the sale was so great that through the Archbishop of Madrid, the matter was referred to the Pope, who ruled that the nuns should sell it for the best offer. Something over 300,000 pesetas was paid for it, and it reached London at the end of 1929. Later it appeared in an exhibition at the Rijksmuseum in Amsterdam, and in 1940 it was shipped to the Art Gallery of Toronto, Canada, for safe-keeping during the Second World War. At the end of the war, the carpet was returned to the United Kingdom, and was then purchased by the well-known carpet manufacturers James Templeton & Co. Ltd, of Glasgow. Templeton's, makers of fine machine-made carpets, and inventors of the Chenille process of weaving, reproduced the design of the Trinitarias carpet in one of their finest Chenille qualities — the 'Abbey' quality, and it proved to be a most successful addition to their range of designs. In 1958 Messrs Templeton sold the Trinitarias carpet to the National Gallery of Victoria, Melbourne, Australia, where it is now housed. Technical details of the carpet are as follows:

size: 10.30 m × 3.40 m (33 ft 9 ins × 11 ft 2 ins)
knot: Persian or Senneh
warps and wefts: cotton
pile: wool — 170 knots to the square inch.

It is not as finely woven as the examples of the period to be seen in the leading museums in Europe and America, nor is it comparable in its structure, as the foundations are of cotton as opposed to the silk of the other museum pieces. However, it deserves special mention because of its condition, which is wonderful for its age, owing no doubt to the cloistered surroundings in which it was housed for centuries. Even the famous Ardebil carpet in the Victoria and Albert Museum, London, which is usually quoted to set the standard for the period, is not a single carpet but the beautifully renovated product of two almost identical carpets.

The firm of Perez (London) Ltd have in their possession a framed fragment [figure 61], together with the original letter dated 26 January 1926, signed by Mr Alfred Brown, Chairman of Vincent Robinson & Co. Ltd, which reads as follows:

I certify the attached fragment of carpet to be a genuine and actual piece of the world famous Ardebil carpet now in the Victoria and Albert, South Kensington, Museum.
The said carpet was imported by this Company into this country in 1886 of which Company I was then a Partner and Director, and still remain so.
The carpet, with its duplicate, was in a delapidated (*sic*) condition when imported and was restored to its present condition by incorporating portions of the second carpet by this Company, in which work I took an active part.

The incredible thing about the carpets of the Sefavi period is the fact that nothing whatever is known about where they were made. Certainly they were made in towns or cities, all within a period of just over a century, during which time there were various wars, particularly against Turkey, and the seat of government must have moved quite a few times as ground was lost or won. It is always assumed that the manufacture of these masterpieces was under the patronage of the reigning Shah, and the names of Shah Tahmasp and Shah Abbas the Great, whose reigns cover most of this period, and who were known to be patrons of the arts, are mainly associated with these pieces.

Actually, they must have been made in properly equipped factories, and if one contemplates the amount of work and the number of people necessary to make even one carpet, the

64 Fine Tabriz carpet. Late nineteenth century: 13 ft 2 ins × 9 ft 5 ins

total number engaged in textile manufacture in those days can only have been counted in thousands.

The wool of many hundreds of sheep had to be sorted, cleaned, scoured and hand-spun into yarn for the pile. Meanwhile the foundation threads for the warps and wefts had to be hand-spun either from cotton or silk. The designer had already been busy and, judging by the results, he was an artist of the first order. The carpets of this Golden Age appear to have broken new ground in design, inasmuch as they seem to have been designed as an entity — that is, the borders were complementary to the field, and the corner decorations within the field were complementary to the centre medallion, where one existed. Hitherto, borders seemed to be made just as a protection for the field, but now

65 Tabriz carpet from the first half of the sixteenth century

there were proper symmetrically designed carpets, all facets of which were in proportion to each other. It has been said that this was an extension of the older art of book-binding, and this may well be so when one contemplates the covers for the manuscripts of those days. Obviously the designers of the day worked with the utmost precision, and the original artist's conception, or cartoon, was laboriously transferred onto squared paper, each square representing a knot, and in the correct colourings, just as is done today in any carpet design studio.

Next on the list of preparatory operations was the dyeing of the yarn. This again was an extremely skilled job, the secrets of which were handed down from father to son. When we look at a sixteenth or seventeenth century piece now, we see a mellowed version of the original colours. In their early days, the colours would have been rather raw to our eyes, but, of course, blended perfectly. The dyes used were naturally of vegetable, mineral or animal origin. The fame of these dyemasters spread far and wide, even into England, as we find recorded by the historian Richard Hakluyt in 1579:

> Certaine directions given by M. Richard Hackluit of the Middle Temple, to M. Morgan Hubblethorne, Dier, sent into Persia 1579 . . . In Persia you shall finde carpets of course thrummed wooll, the best of the World, and excellently coloured; those cities and townes you must repair to, and you must use meanes to learne all the order of the dying of those thrummes, which are so died as neither raine, wine nor yet vineger can staine: and if you may attaine to that cunning, you shall not need to feare dying of cloth: For if the colour holde in yarne and thrumme, it will holde much better in cloth . . . If before you returne you could procure a single good workman in the arte of Turkish carpet making, you should bring the arte into this Realme, and also thereby increase worke to your company.

Unfortunately, we are not informed whether or not Mr Hubblethorne was successful in his quest, but it is highly unlikely. In the old days of 'natural' dyes, the art of dyeing was a family tradition, handed on from father to son, and the actual recipes used were jealously guarded secrets, for on the success of these recipes hung the livelihood of the dyer and his family, and it is not at all probable that he would easily part with them to a stranger – even more so since that stranger was an infidel from a foreign land.

On this score it is interesting to note that there was one occasion when an Indian dyer was persuaded to part with one or two of his recipes, and delightful reading they make. One, for example, started off with instructions to 'take alum and cinnamon, grind and sift light as the light dust of the high hills . . .' Another more prosaic recipe for a good rich red reads:

> Take lac colour and cochineal. Steep from four to six days in the sun, in hot weather for the lesser period, stirring constantly, till a rich deep colour comes where some has stood for a few minutes in a thin glass bottle and settled. Then strain through two cloths, and put in pomegranate rind and good iron filings water. Add mineral acid, steep the wool for thirty-six hours, then boil for three hours, wash well and dry.

The thought of stirring that mixture for from four to six days under the full weight of an Indian sun does not sound like a life of ease, but all this labour merely produced *one* of the colours needed for a carpet. Multiply all this work by twelve or even fifteen and you have some idea of the labour and time that went into the production of some of those Old Masters of the golden age of rug weaving.

After all the preliminary preparations the materials were at last ready for the loom. Looms for hand knotting have not changed much over the centuries. Nomadic people used the horizontal version, and still do so. It is easy to dismantle and move from place to place, and it can easily be re-erected on any small flat area of terrain. However, to make the type of carpet we are reviewing, an upright loom is required, and some pretty long and perfectly straight timbers are necessary. The Ardebil carpet is 17 ft 6 ins wide, so the top and bottom rollers on which the warp threads are wound would have to be somewhat longer than this. For such a size of piece four or five weavers sitting side by side would be about right.

Some years later, after the completed carpet had been taken off the loom, the finishing processes began. Firstly, the carpet had to be cropped. Today, in a modern western factory, a cropping machine does this in a very short time, but in the days of which we are writing, it all had to be done bit by bit with large curved scissors or hand shears. Finally, after a good brushing, the carpet was washed. If possible this took place in a local river or lake, the carpet being left to dry in the sun.

The above procedure has been given in some detail in oder to illustrate the fact that vast armies of highly skilled work people were necessary to turn out these masterpieces, and we still do not know exactly where any of them were made.

With the death of Shah Abbas the Great, a slow decline

66 Kashan carpet of the early twentieth century: 11 ft 10 ins × 8 ft 4 ins

set in which was not to be reversed until well into the nineteenth century. The revival came through two sources. Firstly, the Shah of the reigning Qajar dynasty started to take an interest in the arts at about the middle of the century [figure 37] and, secondly, the merchants of Tabriz found a growing trade in Persian carpets and rugs for export.

Gradually a business with Europe was built up, not only in Tabriz, but in the surrounding area, and in 1883 the first European firm established an office in Sultanabad (now Arak). This was a Manchester firm which exported cotton piece goods to Persia. This firm, Ziegler & Co., had been dealing with Persia for twenty years or more, and already had an office in Tabriz. Apparently they found difficulty in getting their money out of Persia, and it was suggested that they should order carpets for European consumption, the export of which would provide the necessary *per contra* value. Before very long Ziegler & Co. were doing a large business in Persian carpets from Sultanabad, and other places in the area, not only by ordering carpets of traditional sizes and designs, but by cultivating a market in special sizes, and even designs, for the European market. Hitherto carpets had been made in sizes applicable to Persian use, but henceforth, the now familiar sizes were being made for use in rooms of very different shapes. Ziegler's also used softer shades of colour than had been used before, particularly a soft green shade, and although the carpets were not of the best quality, even today one can find a piece in good condition, which could only have been from the looms controlled by this enterprising firm. They were the first Europeans to put their name to a quality of Persian carpet, and even now, long after they liquidated (before the Second World War) an auction room catalogue may still refer to a piece as a 'Ziegler'. Ziegler's were also responsible for obtaining the Ardebil carpet in 1886 from the mosque at Ardebil, together with the second carpet mentioned earlier.

Other European business-houses, particularly German ones, followed Ziegler's lead, and the Americans also sent representatives to place orders with weavers in towns and villages. Meanwhile, the Tabriz merchants had not been idle. They took control of much of the weaving in such distant places as Meshed, Kashan, and Kirman, either by establishing factories or placing orders with weavers on a cottage industry basis. They, too, started to evolve new designs, which could incorporate the new colour schemes wanted in the western world, and the new western sizes.

67 Tabriz carpet of garden design, with inscriptions. Dated in the small centre circle 1325 AH (1907 AD): 13 ft 7 ins × 9 ft 3 ins

Kirman appeared to be the chief attraction for the American market, and although other types of goods were naturally imported into America, the Kirman was one of the most popular, and it still is so today.

All this activity laid the foundations for a very healthy export business which continues today, and now some of the earlier revival pieces have reached the age of mellowness which bring them almost into the antique category.

By the turn of the century some very good Tabriz and

68 Tabriz carpet of 'Portuguese' design. The significance of this design is not understood, nor the reason for the name, although various theories have been given. It has been said that it was executed in the seventeenth century for the Portuguese in Goa, and indeed the sailing ships are manned by Europeans. Whatever the significance, the design appears to be of a volcanic island, the red centre being the crater. The next band of colour is cream, or natural, which could represent the snow line. Then comes green, the tree line, and finally a light brown colour representing sand, before the sea. 19 ft 7 ins × 9 ft 10 ins

Kirman pieces were being made, and those still in existence today can command good prices in world markets. Armenian and Persian dealers settled in America and Europe, and placed orders back home for special qualities, sizes and designs, and some dealers even today incorporate a symbol or signature unobtrusively placed in a corner on one of the borders, or at the edge of the field, in qualities made exclusively for them which have proved successful.

Shortly after the turn of the century, another innovation was introduced into England. It was known that different waters had different effects upon materials such as wool, and after weaving many carpets were immersed in rivers or dammed-up streams known to be effective, before being offered to the consumer. Certain waters imparted a kind of silky sheen to certain types of wool, and took excess colour out of the carpet, mellowing it somewhat. It became increasingly important to find ways of doing this in the latter part of the nineteenth century and the early part of the twentieth, because genuine old goods became scarce, and it was their mellow colourings that were wanted by the western world.

How then to make the harsh new colours of the contemporary rugs look something like the old ones? The dealers in Tabriz, Constantinople (Istanbul) and other towns tried many ways, one of which was to place the rugs in public places for the daily traffic to trample on them, after which, when the surplus dirt had been removed, the colours would at least have become much softer. The local answers to the problem were interesting enough, but not for the quantity of goods now demanded. The solution was soon to be put on a gigantic commercial basis by an Armenian who set up a chemical washing plant in London in 1907. His name was Shahinian, and for many years he had the monopoly for this process, being the only 'chemical washer' in Europe. No need now to find a suitable water or other local means to obtain the required finish for a particular rug or, indeed, for a particular market. Mr Shahinian had the answer in his little bottles.

Carpets were made under contract in every producing country of suitable yarns and dyes for the type of wash they were destined to undergo, and it was this processing enterprise which helped in no small way to make the London transit market the largest in the world, and the centre of world trade in Oriental rugs and carpets. The warehousing for this vast quantity of goods was, and still is, carried out at the Cutler Street Bonded warehouses of the Port of Lon-

69 Silk Heriz rug: 6 ft 1 in × 4 ft 6 ins

70 Kirman rug of the nineteenth century, with the pine or leaf design associated with shawls. In the early nineteenth century a large business grew up in Paisley, Scotland, making shawls with this design

don Authority in the city of London, known colloquially as the PLA or just the 'Docks', the latter name being a misnomer, as they are some distance from the river. The actual location of these cold, dark, thick-walled warehouses is very roughly a kind of triangle with sides on Bishopsgate, Houndsditch and Middlesex Street (the famous Petticoat Lane). The description cold and dark refers only to the buildings, which are very old and were once associated with Clive of India. Go inside these buildings, and a world of colour bursts forth. Here are rugs and carpets from every producing country, old, new, washed, unwashed, and they are all recorded in the stock books, piece by piece, by the Port of London Authority. Each piece has a PLA stock number, and a PLA size, which is accepted by everyone as being correct. The individual traders do, of course, keep records too, but when the carpets enter or leave the Bonded premises, it is the PLA record which is used.

London did not, however, remain the only transit port; Germany in particular became an important market, and today it is by far the biggest consumer of Persian goods in Europe.

From the early years of this century the American market also developed, mainly, in the first place, with old goods but later, as these became somewhat scarce, a business was created, particularly with Kirman, in a special type of texture and design which today is easily identified as an 'American Kirman'.

The Persians have always been masters of design, not only in rugs but in every conceivable form of art. In our particular field, ever since the Golden Age, any Persian carpet has always been of a 'complete' design, that is, a design in which every motif is in the right proportion to the whole. We are speaking, of course, of town carpets as distinct from tribal or rural cottage pieces, many of which, although masterpieces of their kind, were not the ultimate result of the artist's conception. The towns from which these exquisitely designed carpets emanated are not many in number, and a few words about their turbulent history will show that much dedication was required to carry on with artistic life in the face of the troubles to which they were subjected.

*Tabriz*

The mere geographical position of this city ensured for it an importance above the average. Situated in the north-west corner of Persia it is the gateway to Turkey in the west and

71 Modern Isfahan rug: 6 ft 6 ins × 4 ft 9 ins

Caucasia in the north, well-placed as a trading centre during peacetime and a very important bastion in wartime. During the eleventh century when Persia was conquered by the Seljuk Turks, these invaders settled in the province of Azerbaijan, of which Tabriz is the principal city, and they introduced the Turkish language, a dialect of which is still spoken there. It was in the thirteenth century, however, that Tabriz became a capital city under the Mongols. For three hundred years it survived a long series of wars from all quarters, but at the end of the sixteenth century Shah Abbas the Great moved his capital to Isfahan, which is in the centre of the country, and therefore less vulnerable.

It has been thought that the great carpets of the sixteenth century were made in Tabriz, but this is hardly possible because firstly, in addition to being Turkish speaking, the weavers of Tabriz, and indeed of the whole of Azerbaijan, use the Turkish or Ghiordes knot, and the sixteenth century masterpieces are all constructed with the Persian or Senneh knot. Secondly, the Ardebil carpet is dated 1539/40 and it is assumed that this is the year it was either completed, or very near to it. If that is so, the piece was being made a few years previously in 1534, the year when Tabriz had been taken by the Ottomans, and the capital temporarily removed to Kasvin. It seems improbable that the court manufactory was taken away and set up again during the making of this carpet.

Like the rest of the country, Tabriz was subject to the gentle decline in textile art, but the merchants of the city traded in a multitude of commodities with whichever conqueror came along, and by the middle of the nineteenth century it was again a very wealthy city. As foreign trade expanded, so Tabriz prospered, the merchants bringing goods from all corners of Persia for onward transmission to Constantinople (Istanbul) and thence to Europe and America. Once it became the practice to weave custom-made carpets for the various overseas markets, often under European supervision, Tabriz weavers made vast quantities, and still do so. Unfortunately they have set their quantities above their qualities, and although between the two world wars some very high quality pieces were produced, very low qualities were, alas, also introduced, and even today some very poor carpets come from that city. To their credit, however, it must be said that high-grade carpets can still be obtained, but not enough of them are seen on the market, probably because of their price.

Before we leave Tabriz, it should be mentioned that, unlike all other Persian weavers, the weavers of Tabriz do not tie the knots with their fingers, but with a knife with a hook on the end. They can work astonishingly quickly with this instrument. The blade is, of course, used to cut the yarn after the knot has been made.

## Isfahan

This beautiful city, right in the heart of the country, made a worthy capital when Shah Abbas the Great moved here in 1590. There is ample documentary evidence that he established a large court manufactory here, and it is on this evidence that many sixteenth- and seventeenth-century carpets are credited with having been made here. Certainly there are to this day many antique carpets referred to as Isfahan [figure 51], but whether they all came from the looms set up by Shah Abbas or not is debatable. Shah Abbas died in 1629 and from then on until the Afghan invasion in 1722 a decline set in, so it can be assumed that the period of greatness only lasted about forty or fifty years.

Revival of the craft did not begin in Isfahan until after the First World War, and today Isfahan rugs and carpets are purely commercial and not very attractive; there is something about the finish which belies their beautiful designs. Their colours, too, appear to lack the blend of shades which the designs deserve.

## Kirman

Situated in the south, this very old city is on the southern trade route to India. There is no record of carpet weaving here in the early days, although some authorities attribute a

72 Modern Kashan carpet: 11 ft 10 ins × 8 ft 4 ins

73 Silk Heriz rug: 6 ft 6 ins × 4 ft 5 ins

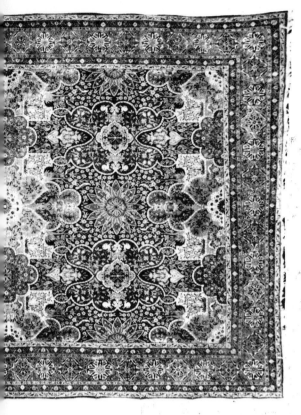

few sixteenth-century examples to this city. It is known, however, that there was carpet weaving in this city during the reign of Shah Abbas the Great and subsequently, and that carpets were being exported to India during the reign of the Mogul Emperor Akbar. As with all Persian history, a decline set in, and nothing is heard of Kirman again until the nineteenth century. It was not in carpets, however, that the name became known to the western world, but in shawls, which were strangely enough of similar design to the famous Kashmir shawls, with the well known pine-cone or leaf design which, in Britain, is associated with the Paisley shawl [figure 70].

The Kirmanis are the masters of designs in floral form. They are adept at producing the most intricate designs of all. In the nineteenth century, when their products started to attract the attention of the western world due to the enterprise of the Tabriz merchants, they were constructed of fine wool, very closely woven, and the pile was cropped short, giving extremely good definition of design [figures 28 and 52]. The multitude of colours employed gave an overall picture of quiet efficiency, not matched in the carpets of the time. America, however, wanted a more durable and heavier textured product, and gradually the Kirman weave took on a different appearance. In design they still retained the hallmark of Kirman draughtsmanship, but a high pile was employed which took away some of the precision of the definition seen in the earlier pieces. The colours were also somewhat crude, but chemical washing took care of that problem, so that by the nineteen-twenties a carpet had evolved which was known in the trade as the 'American Kirman'. America was, and probably still is, the largest market for Kirmans, so no blame should attach to the makers for providing the requirements for a profitable market, even though some of the artistry dies in so doing. After the Second World War, the market demanded designs with a French flavour, and these they got also. Today, Kirmans are good, sound pieces in the main, their crowning glory lying in the ingenuity of their designers but, with the introduction of modern chemical dyes, the glorious harmony of their exquisite soft tones has inevitably been lost.

### Kashan

This city has as good a claim as any of the places where the Ardebil and other carpets of the same period might have been made. It is known that carpets and other textiles were

76 An unusual design from Khorassan. The corner and border motifs are variations of the pine or leaf design seen in the Kirman rug

74 (*opposite top*) Kashan carpet of the early twentieth century: 15 ft 3 ins × 10 ft 3 ins

75 (*opposite bottom*) So-called 'Herat' carpet: 14 ft 7 ins × 6 ft 7 ins. The field design of this piece is used with some variation in many parts of Persia. It is known as the 'Herati' design

woven here in the sixteenth and seventeenth centuries, and Maksoud, whose name graces the inscription on the Ardebil carpet, came from here, or at least signed himself as Maksoud of Kashan. If this were to be confirmed, a lot of words written in the last fifty years or so would become superfluous. Be that as it may, there are Kashans still in existence from these early days, but as in everywhere else in Persia, the art declined after the death of Shah Abbas the Great and did not recover again until the nineteenth century.

The woollen carpets of Kashan from the middle of the nineteenth century are still looked for in the markets of the world. Made with extremely fine wool and mellowed with age, they are magnificent specimens and now have a wonderful natural sheen or glazure on the pile which could not be emulated by chemical washers. This is due to the type of wool used in Kashan in those days. Of later years, and up to today, Kashan still turns out good quality pieces [figure 72], but with two reservations: firstly, the yarns used are in no way comparable to those used fifty to a hundred years ago and secondly there is a lack of variety in the designs.

Kashan also produces silk rugs and carpets, and here the modern product faces the criticism of sameness of design, coupled with a harshness of colour which one is anxious not to interfere with lest the colours should be disturbed. In other words, the dyes may be good, but they do not show it with confidence. However, the silk Kashans of the nineteenth and early twentieth centuries have stood the test of time and when in good condition are much sought after for their beauty [figure 72].

### Meshed and Herat

If it can be said that Tabriz is situated at the crossroads of the west, Meshed occupies the same position in the east. The political capital of Persia for a brief period in the eighteenth century, it has for centuries been the religious capital and a centre of pilgrimage for the whole country, for here is the tomb of Imam Riza, the eighth Imam of the Moslem faith who was martyred there in the ninth century. Herat is, of course, in Afghanistan, but any discussion involving Eastern Persia must inevitably include this formerly Persian city. The reason for this is that examples from the sixteenth century to the eighteenth which are still in existence, and designated 'East Persian', are attributed not to Meshed, which has a long history of textile weaving, but to Herat, although no evidence exists that weaving was ever carried

67

77 Bakhtiari runner: 13 ft 3 ins × 3 ft 10 ins

on there. Indeed, one of the most common Persian designs, woven in many parts of the country in various forms, is known as the 'Herati' design [figure 75]. Somehow the name of Herat became associated with a particular type of carpet in those early days, but it is never used for the modern product.

The nineteenth-century revival of the carpet saw the

78 Part silk Qum rug: 7 ft × 4 ft 10 ins

79 Detail of Bijar carpet: 16 ft 4 ins × 10 ft

emergence of what is known as the Khorassan carpet [figure 76] not necessarily made in Meshed, but in the province of that name, of which Meshed is the principal city. Khorassans were not, however, commercial pieces in the sense in which we regard the term, even the sizes being of the old Persian proportions—long and narrow. Mesheds as we now know them are made in western sizes for export, and they come in various qualities. In general they have a somewhat sombre appearance, not suitable for chemical washing, and the yarn lacks the lustre associated with other Persian weaves [figure 80]. Both Turkish and Persian knotting is employed here. Carpets made with the former are actually named Turkbaff, and not Meshed, which definition is used for the Persian knotted variety. The word *Turkbaff* means 'Turkish knot', while *Farsibaff* refers to the Persian knot.

So far, only the largest cities of Persia have been discussed, those in which the art of design has played a big part in their development over the centuries, and which have placed Persia in the forefront of carpet production in the Orient. There are, however, some smaller places, possibly not so well known, which have also made, and still make, their contribution to the overall picture of the country which produces a greater variety of carpets than any other.

### *Heriz* and *Ghorovan*

From these two towns between Tabriz and the west coast of the Caspian Sea, and their immediate surroundings, come the unmistakable types of carpets known the world over by these names. They are of coarse weave, but extremely tough, usually with centre medallion designs, very angular, in shades of rust or rusty red. These towns have no history going back to the Sefavi period, and, indeed, antique carpets are not found at all, but the older pieces, fifty to seventy years old, are usually called Old Ghorovan. Also from this area come the Karajah strips and scatter rugs of colourings similar to the Heriz.

### *Qum* and *Nain*

Both these towns are on the main road skirting the western edge of the desert, the road from the capital, Teheran, to Kirman, the old route to India. Both started weaving carpets in the decade before the Second World War. Both produce fine rugs. Here the similarities end.

Qum is an important town in the religious sense, with many pilgrims visiting its shrine every year, for here are buried

80 Modern Meshed carpet: 14 ft 4 ins × 15 ft 5 ins

some of the Sefavi and Qajar rulers. Strangely enough, the town has no weaving history. When weaving commenced in Qum, it was not with the normal traditional designs that the weavers worked. The designers created new forms, based on the traditional patterns but in small all-over designs, as opposed to the designs of Kashan [figure 78].

Nain was important for the weaving of woollen cloth until it declined in the nineteen-thirties, when the weavers turned their energies to rugs. From here come now some of the finest rugs ever woven in Persia. They are made from finely spun wool, which is short cropped, giving a clarity of design unmatched elsewhere. They also sometimes weave with part silk pile, giving a glittering effect which results in the illusion that the rug is embossed. Always expensive, never seen in profusion, if any modern Persian rugs are to create the treasures of tomorrow, those from Nain will be among the leaders.

Some further names should be recounted because of the contribution they have made historically, or for their place in the modern world of hand-knotted fabrics. Firstly, the carpets of Joshaghan, just off the main road south of Kashan, have remained almost identical in design — and one design only — for over two hundred years. Not many are turned out today, but those which find their way onto the market are quite unmistakable [figure 80]. The name of Senneh will not be found on Persian maps, the town being called Sanandaj, but in carpet lore Senneh is the name given to the particular type of knot used by the Persian weavers as distinct from the Turkish one. Why the name of Senneh was given to this knot is a mystery, because the town itself lies in the heart of the Kurdish area of Persia, where the people not only speak Turkish, but naturally use the Turkish knot in their weaving as well. A possible answer may be that the rugs of Senneh are so finely woven that early western observers, not checking their facts, were misled into thinking that only the Persian knot could have produced such weaving. It would be a natural mistake to make, because the Senneh is very fine, with a peculiarly lustreless pile, cropped much shorter than any other Persian rug [figures 83 and 86]. Not many are made now, and it is the semi-antique rugs which are in demand, and these are naturally becoming scarcer as time goes by.

In contrast, the Bijar carpet from the town of that name in the neighbourhood of Sanandaj is, and always was, a robust effort, solid, in many cases so hard it could hardly be

81 Typically designed modern Heriz carpet: 11 ft 2 ins × 7 ft 8 ins

82 Silk Heriz rug with inscription: 6 ft 1 in × 4 ft 4 ins. Dated 1282 AH (1865 AD)

folded for packing [figure 79]. Sultanabad or Arak, to give the town its modern name, has been mentioned previously as being the place where Messrs Ziegler & Co. began business in 1883. Today the various trade-named carpets such as Muscabad, Mahal, Saruk and Sultanabad are still being produced in this area. From here also come the dainty Malayer rugs as well as the hard-wearing Fereghan carpets.

It is difficult to know which names to leave out in dealing with the above areas. The goods from all these places, and many more villages in the surrounding countryside, are now marketed in Hamadan, which is a large city where a number of European exporting houses have offices and buying agents to gather carpets from an area comprising some hundreds of villages. Hamadan has had its moments historically, but not in the art of weaving. Today it is one of the

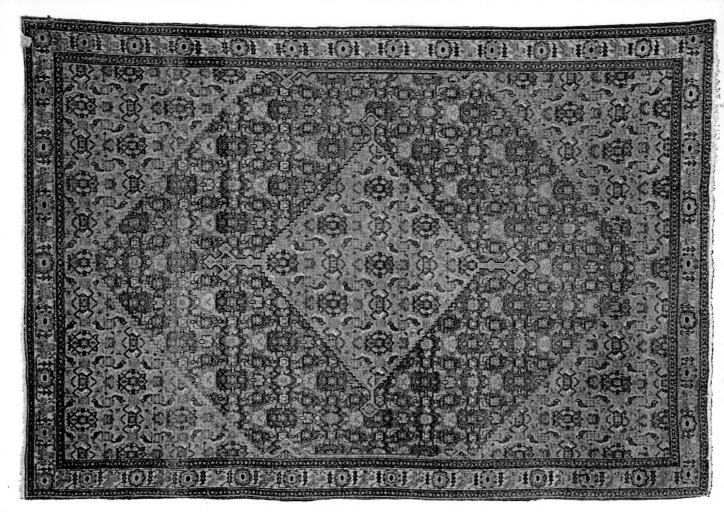

83 Senneh rug: 6 ft 9 ins × 4 ft 6 ins

most important cities in Persia for the collection and for-
warding of goods to America and Europe [figure 88]. Also
from this area come the unmistakable rugs and runners
known as Sarabend. The design of these is always a version
of the pine cone or leaf design [figure 90].

Cities, towns and villages, all make rugs and carpets, but
there are also the tribal areas, which cannot be left out of
any discourse on this subject.

The Bakhtiari tribe is probably the best known in Persia,
and one of the largest. Rugs from their area, which is west
of Isfahan, are in a rather coarse weave, often in garden or
panel designs. Very colourful, these rugs are not tribal at
all in character, having a more formal appearance than one
would normally associate with a nomadic people [figure 77].
The reason for this lies in the fact that these rugs are not
made by the Bakhtiari tribe proper, but by the villagers in
an area where a section of their people settled more than a
hundred years ago, since when they have led a sedentary

84 Tekke Bokhara rug: 7 ft
10 ins × 4 ft

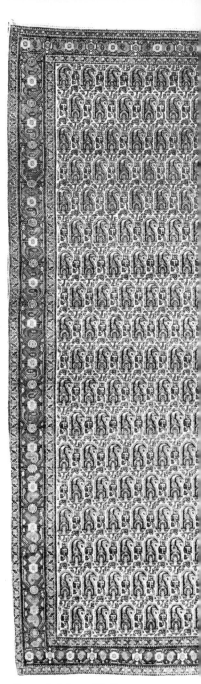

85 Joshaghan: 10 ft 2 ins × 7 ft

existence, in contrast to the main tribe which still lives a nomadic life.

Another large tribe, this time really nomadic, is the Afshari. These people are of Turkish origin, and they only moved into Persia in the sixteenth century. Their habitat is the area between Shiraz and Kirman, and their rugs are sold on both markets. Also sold on the Shiraz market are the products of the Quashqai tribe, inhabitants of the Fars district, to the north of Shiraz.

86 (*above centre*) Senneh rug with a variation of the pine or leaf design: 6 ft 7 ins × 4 ft 6 ins

87 (*above right*) An unusual Fereghan rug, as the pile is of silk: 6 ft 6 ins × 4 ft 4 ins

The other important tribal area from which rugs emanate is in the north-east of the country. Here are the wandering Beloutchi people, who provide the cheap dark purplish-red and black coloured rugs known throughout the world as Beloutch rugs. The Tekkes and Yamouts inhabit the frontier territory common to Persia and Turkestan. From these people come the so-called Bokhara rugs, which will be more fully discussed in the next chapter.

75

90 (*below*) Sarabend runner: 9 ft 10 ins ×
3 ft 4 ins. A further variation of the pine or
leaf design

91 (*bottom*) Detail of Agra carpet: 14 ft 9 ins
× 11 ft 3 ins

# TURKESTAN

ALMOST EVERYONE has heard of a Bokhara rug, but it is possibly true to say that hardly anyone knows anything more about the wonderful knotted fabrics which come from the two Soviet Republics of Turkmenskaya and Uzbekskaya.

This area, bounded in the south by Persia and Afghanistan, and by the Caspian Sea in the west, is the original home of the Turks, and turns out many items in knotted pile other than rugs. All their products are made for home use, or perhaps one should say tent use, because these are a nomadic people, and there is no organized industry as in other rug-producing countries. Although on the ancient trade route from China, there is no record of rug weaving earlier than the nineteenth century; yet the sheer artistry and technique of these rugs can only lead one to believe that they stem from a long ancestry. The probable reason for our lack of knowledge about them is the fact that for some centuries Turkestan was isolated from the rest of the world, only opening up somewhat in the last quarter of the nineteenth century after the Russian conquest. Nothing of interest historically will have survived, as the products of Turkestan were always purely functional, and although hand-woven textiles, particularly knotted ones, are extremely hard wearing, the constant use of them by a tribe always on the move is hardly conducive to preservation.

Before giving consideration to the various tribes in Turkestan, it may be as well to dispose of some ill-founded descriptions which may confuse the issue. For instance, it is general practice to refer to all products from this area, and also from other areas, not necessarily adjoining but using the same designs, as Bokhara. There must also be many owners of rugs who bought them with the rather grand labels of 'Royal Bokhara' or 'Princess Bokhara'. These descriptions are the figment of a rug dealer's mind, to obtain a better price by upgrading rugs with non-essential names. It

92 Turkoman saddle bags

93 Turkoman tent band

94 (*below*) Yamout Bokhara tent bag

should be noted that the city of Bokhara is not a rug-making town, but the market for many of the pieces made by the various Turkoman tribes.

It has been mentioned above that many items other then rugs are made in this district. Tent bands, woven with the design in pile on a flat hand-woven canvas foundation which gives an embossed effect, are used as a kind of frieze round the walls of a tent [figure 93]. Their length is usually about 42 ft, which would doubtless be equivalent to the perimeter of a normal sized tent, although some much longer ones have been found. Gun and water bottle covers are other examples of the great variety of objects made with knotted pile. More commonplace in western countries, however, are tent bags, camel bags and cushions, all gracefully worked by these strange nomadic people for their comfort in what must be a very hard country [figure 92]. The largest tribe is that known as Tekke [figures 84 and 98]. These people inhabit the southern part of Turkestan and part of the province of Khorassan, over the political border in Persia, as also do the Yamouts, who weave the finest qualities [figure 94]. Other large tribes are the Salors and the Pendehs. All these have their little characteristics in design, and strictly speaking

95 Eastern Turkestan rug (Samarkand): 7 ft 9 ins × 4 ft 7 ins

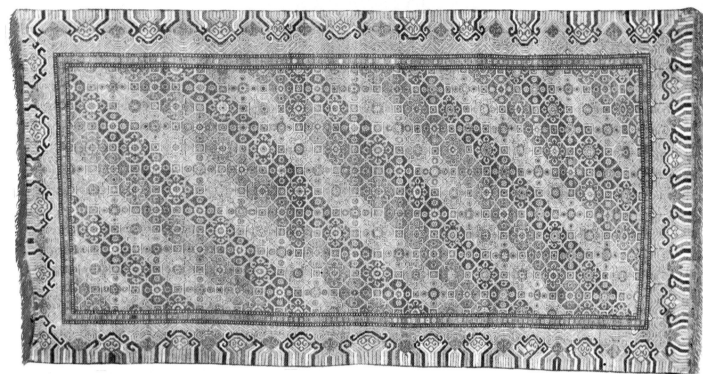

96 (*above*) Eastern Turkestan rug (Samarkand): 9 ft 4 ins × 4 ft 10 ins

97 (*above top*) Silk pile Kashgar small carpet from Eastern Turkestan: 10 ft 11 ins × 5 ft 5 ins

98 Tekke Turkoman (Bokhara) carpet of the late nineteenth century: 10 ft 8 ins × 7 ft

any Turkoman rug should be prefixed by the tribal name. The one exception is the Hatchli, which is a design in the form of a cross, made by various tribes, and reputedly used as a tent doorway.

The name Beshir is applied to a particular kind of Turkoman rug. It is not a tribal piece, as is the case with the others enumerated above. There is some doubt as to where the name originates, one being that it is a *sept* or branch of a large tribe. Beshirs do not contain the conventional Turkoman octagon forms, and a further characteristic is that very large carpets are occasionally found, which is not so in the case of the other Turkoman pieces, the largest size being about 13 ft × 10 ft. One other form of weaving has to be mentioned: the pileless fabric known elsewhere as Kelim, but here referred to as 'Palas'. These pieces are used as wall hangings, settee covers and divan or table coverings.

All Turkoman textile products feature the blood red ground colour which is not found anywhere else. Apart from being a very acceptable colour to western eyes, it is the natural colour for a nomadic people to use in such a cold and desolate area as Turkestan.

Of course, the foregoing was primarily about Western Turkestan, and although the political boundaries do not coincide, there is a region which must be termed, for the purposes of this book, Eastern Turkestan. The marketing centre for this district is Samarkand, something over 100 miles east of Bokhara; although it is, like Bokhara, in the Soviet Republic of Uzbekskaya, the design is purely Chinese in character [figures 95 and 96]. It is true that Chinese designs found their way westwards, even into Turkey, and many of the so-called Turkish designs can be traced back to Chinese origin, but Eastern Turkestan appears to be a no-man's-land between East and West, and the designs encountered in this market, while retaining their Chinese motifs, have also a flavour of the West about them. It is a vast area, and rugs from Khotan, Kashgar, and Yarkand are collectively called Samarkand in the markets of the West [figure 97]. One deplorable practice must be mentioned here, which does not enhance the reputation of this district which produces such original pieces. It is well known that as in Western Turkestan no proof of antiquity can be established. However, in Europe, and particularly in England, there has grown up a practice of washing the rather brash colourings out of these primitive, but not old pieces, the resulting appearance — almost completely colourless — being much favoured by certain interior decorators. While there can be a certain charm in a room decorated with a carpet treated in this manner, the intrinsic value of the piece has been utterly destroyed, and its wearing qualities very seriously impaired. Unfortunately, too, these pieces are often represented to be much older than they are.

# THE MARGINAL AREAS

ALTHOUGH THIS CHAPTER is confined to the less important producing areas, historically speaking, this does not mean to say that they have not made any significant mark on the craft. On the contrary, it will be seen that some excellent pieces came from these places, but in some cases there is a lack of authenticity, while in others there is a lack of continuity. It is felt that the best way to deal with this section

99 Old Chinese silk rug: 8 ft 3 ins × 5 ft 4 ins

101 Old Chinese rug: 6 ft 9 ins × 4 ft 4 ins

would be to follow the ancient trade routes, starting in the far east with China, and travelling westwards.

## CHINA

The earliest Chinese carpets known are from the seventeenth century. This suggests that the Chinese were late starters in the textile field, but it is inconceivable that this country, so advanced in other arts and crafts, should have been behind in this technique which was so prevalent in other parts of the Orient. According to the records, the custom of using carpets as furnishings began as early as 1122 BC, but of course this has never been substantiated by even the smallest practical example. In this context we are, of course, speaking of China proper. Elsewhere in this book it will be seen that the earliest known knotted rug was found near the Outer Mongolian border, but this is attributed to Persia and not to China. Certainly Chinese motifs found their way into the early rugs of Turkey and the Caucasus, which also suggests that this vast country was participating in the craft much earlier than is supposed.

The main centre of production in the nineteenth century appears to have been Pekin, and even today we can find carpets which are attributed to this city [figure 100]. Completely Chinese in character, many with a blue ground colour, they are very different from the modern Chinese product. Exporting carpets from China only started in 1850 and since then the product has undergone many changes to satisfy the appetite of the West. Production is now centred in Tientsin

102 Girdlers' Company Carpet, made in the royal factory at Lahore: 24 ft × 7 ft 6 ins

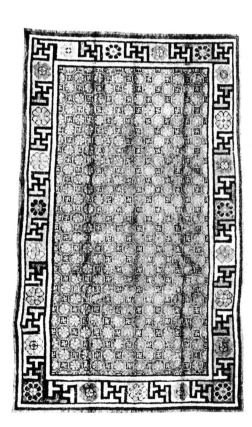

103 Old Ningsia rug: 8 ft 6 ins × 5 ft 6 ins

where, since the nineteen-twenties, a fine yarn, high pile carpet has been made which necessitates chemical washing, and the magnificent silky sheen and carved effect gives a most luxurious appearance to this latest development in Oriental art. A further innovation, made in Hong Kong, is a kind of tufted carpet with a latexed backing. As this is not a traditional weave, such products have not been considered in this volume.

Carpets have appeared which are classified as Sinkiang and Ningsia [figure 103], but these are from areas which could be considered to belong more to Eastern Turkestan than to China, as also would the carpets of Tibet.

One type of knotted rug from China must be mentioned here, as it does not appear in any other country. This is the Pillar rug, made long and very narrow, to surround pillars. This is so skilfully executed that when the rug has been wound spirally around a pillar, the design, hitherto piece-meal, suddenly becomes a coherent whole.

## INDIA

As far as is known, carpets were not actually made in India until the time of the Empire of the Great Moguls in the sixteenth century, although before this they had been imported from Persia, particularly from Kirman, which is not surprising when it is considered that Kirman was the last large Persian city on the trade route to India.

When weaving began in India it was with Persian weavers reputedly imported by Akbar, with the consent of Shah Abbas of Persia, who was his contemporary. The weaving was centred on Agra and Lahore, and, as may be surmised, the designs had a distinctly Persian flavour about

87

104 Agra jail carpet: 14 ft 10 ins × 9 ft

them. Later, while retaining some Persian influence, Indian designers developed their own ideas, the result being a pleasing contrast between the two schools of design.

Early examples from the sixteenth and seventeenth centuries cannot be readily identified as coming from a particular place, and the general tendency is to call any Indian of that period either an Agra or Indo-Persian. There is, in London, however, one Indian carpet, fully documented and known to have been made in the Royal Factory at Lahore [figure 102]. It is in the possession of the Worshipful Company of Girdlers in the city of London, and it was presented to them by Robert Bell, Master of the Company, at the expiry of his second term of office in 1634.

The minutes of the Girdlers Company of 12 August 1634 read: 'Also, at this Court, Mr. Robert Bell did present a very faire long Turkey Carpitt, with the Company's Arms thereon, which he freely gave to the use of this Company as a remembrance of his love.'

The carpet, 24 ft × 7 ft 6 ins, was made to lay on the original Court Room table of the Girdlers Company, which was destroyed in the Great Fire of London in 1666; the design incorporates the Coat of Arms of the Company, two panels bearing Robert Bell's initials, and at each end of the field, Bell's Coat of Arms.

Robert Bell was a prominent member of the East India Company from the time of its foundation in 1600, and a rather long entry is given in the minutes of this Company for 2 April 1634 to the carpet, which it states was made in Lahore. The reason for the entry is because there was a dispute about payment. It appears that the Company was charged with the cost of manufacture and endeavoured to recover the money from Bell. He stated that he had already settled the account personally. The dispute was never resolved, and later in the same year the directors of the East India Company apparently allowed the matter to drop. The interesting thing about this particular carpet is that here is a 'Turkey Carpitt', of Persian design and knotting, undoubtedly made in India. The reference to Turkey is understood when we realize that all Oriental carpets entering England at that time, no matter where they were made, were referred to as such.

Some rather heavy pile Indian carpets come on to the market as 'Jail' carpets. It is known that in the last century prisoners, particularly at Agra and Jaipur, were given the task of making extremely tough carpets, and the story goes

105 (*above*) 'Indo-Isfahan' rug, probably
from Kashmir. Wool and silk pile on silk
foundation: 4 ft 3 ins × 1 ft 10 ins. Approximately 2600 knots to the square inch

106 (*above right*) Modern picture mat – fine
Indian: 2 ft × 1 ft 6 ins

that good weavers were resentenced at the end of their term,
on any pretext that could be found, in order to finish the job
they were on [figure 104].

Since those days, India has remained a carpet producing

107 A 'Bulgarian' Kirman carpet made between the two world wars

country, and even today some pieces of excellent quality are made there.

The sub-continent is now split of course, but for the purposes of this volume, the products of Pakistan and Kashmir will be discussed under the heading of India. The former country now makes very finely-knotted rugs, chemically washed, many of them with Turkoman designs and colours. Kashmir has been a producing country for many years, and in addition to the embroideries for which it is justly famous [figure 108] some exceedingly finely woven pieces have been made there.

The example shown here [figure 105] is in the possession of the author, and it was reputedly made about sixty years ago. Because of the fine knotting, it could only have been made by a child, as it is impossible to imagine such dexterity from adult fingers. Woven on silk warps, with a small amount of silk in the wool pile, the knotting is between fifty and fifty-two per inch each way. This makes about 2600 knots to the square inch, and it is undoubtedly one of the finest knotted examples ever seen. The design is a perfect reproduction, in miniature, of a sixteenth-century Isfahan carpet and, although measuring only 4 ft 3 ins × 1 ft 10 ins, it contains as many knots as an average Oriental carpet twenty times the size. In point of fact this carpet is a miniature reproduction in the real sense of the word, for it was what could best be termed a scaled-down reproduction, knot for knot, of an original.

An interesting sidelight is that this particular rug was exhibited by Messrs Perez, of London, at an exhibition of European and Oriental Carpets at the Royal Water Colour Society's Galleries, London, in 1946. The rug was displayed in a glass cabinet with miniature furniture placed on it, the latter having been made by disabled ex-servicemen of the Star and Garter Home, Richmond, in aid of whom the exhibition had been promoted. The glass cabinet was not quite long enough for the rug to lie flat, and it was therefore curled over at one end. On visiting the exhibition, Her late Majesty Queen Mary suggested that a magnifying glass should be provided, as the knotting was so fine that it could not be seen properly with the naked eye.

## EGYPT

This country, which shares with Peru, Turkestan and Siberia a climate which can preserve textiles almost indefinitely, has never revealed knotted pile fabrics of earlier date than about the fourth century AD. These are not, however, of the right weave to be classified as Oriental rugs, as the knotting is rather coarse and the pile consists of uncut loops. Some authorities claim that the pile was cut, but as many pieces still contain a looped pile it is a fair contention that it was wear rather than the weavers' shears which made the separation. They resemble Turkish towels in appearance. Specimens can be seen in a number of museums featuring Egyptian art.

Carpets are mentioned as having been used in Court circles in the twelfth century, but we do not know if they were made in Egypt or even if they were knotted. In the Mameluke period, however, carpets were actually made in Cairo, and the art of manufacture stemmed from Persia and not Turkey, as the knotting used is Persian.

Unfortunately these pieces, of which there are a number in various museums, have tended to be attributed to Damascus, which is totally wrong, because there is no evidence that carpets were ever made in Syria. The explanation may be that there is some resemblance between the effect of the peculiar designs and colours of these pieces, and damask, a cloth also used in that period, particularly in Venice from where it was exported to the rest of Europe.

Always geometric in design, these Cairo or Mameluke pieces have neither forerunners nor copiers. They appear to have been made only during the period up until the conquest which brought Egypt under the Ottoman Empire in 1517. From then onwards a change of style set in, due no doubt to the demands of the Turkish Court, as the new style, while following the old weaving techniques, featured designs somewhat akin to the Persian Court manufacture, that is, properly proportioned pieces, with corner pieces matching the medallion; but they lacked the overall grandeur of the Persian examples owing to the inferior draughtsmanship employed [figure 109].

What kind of carpets Cardinal Wolsey got in reply to his demand for 'Damascene' carpets will never be known. In June 1518 he asked the Venetian Ambassador for some pieces, in return for which he would 'take him before the Council and obtain audience for his arguments in regard to the repeal of the duties of Candian wines imported into England by the Venetian traders'. At the end of that year he got seven pieces. His next demand, still with the repeal of the wine duties contingent upon it, was for a hundred 'Damascene' carpets. This was in 1519. We do not know if

108 Kashmir embroidered rug: 5 ft × 3 ft 6 ins. Note the Royal cypher at the foot of the piece. Made for the Coronation of Queen Elizabeth II

91

he received them all, but we do know that sixty carpets arrived for him from Antwerp, which he graciously accepted.

As with all the other producing countries a decline set in, but much earlier than with the others, as from the seventeenth century nothing more is heard of Egyptian carpets, and there was no revival in the nineteenth century.

## THE BALKAN COUNTRIES

Flat-woven Kelims have been woven in all the countries of the Balkans for centuries, but their supplies of knotted pile rugs came from Turkey, which is not surprising, as all these countries were provinces of the Ottoman Empire.

The weaving of Kelims has continued, the earlier eastern designs eventually introducing some concessions to western ideas, particularly in the use of flowers, as these countries became Europeanized. In the twentieth century, however, knotted carpets have been produced in most of the Balkan countries, but only as an exporting medium, and today the carpets of Bulgaria, Hungary and Roumania compete in the world markets with the Persian product. Bulgaria has in recent years introduced carpets with classical Persian designs, made with a fine worsted yarn, chemically washed, but with an appearance at least matching most of the contemporary Persian carpets, and at very competitive prices [figure 107]. Whether these rugs will stand the test of time or not is debatable, but for the middle of the twentieth century they look worthy of their cost.

Greece was somewhat apart from her neighbours. In the latter part of the nineteenth century, some Turkish weavers set up their looms and started to make carpets something like those of Isparta in Turkey. These pieces, unwashed but made with a rather glossy fine wool with long pile, graced the late Victorian drawing-rooms of England. For the first time, special designing was used, with open plain fields, to attract the English buyer, and rather than definite colours, pastel shades were used — surely the forerunner of the 'Super-Washed' Chinese carpet of today.

The vogue lasted well into the nineteen-twenties, and even today there are some old Sparta carpets still being used, albeit a little bit out of date in modern furnishing schemes. It would appear that the name 'Sparta' is not in fact derived from the ancient Greek kingdom of that name, but is a corruption of 'Isparta' or 'Isbarta', the town in Asia Minor from which the originals came.

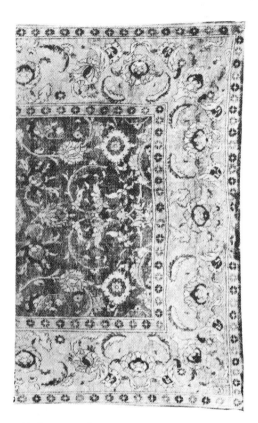

109 Ottoman Cairene rug ('Damascus')

## SPAIN

This purely European country, but with a history of Moorish rule for some hundreds of years, warrants a place in any volume of Oriental rug art for two reasons. The first is that here was the gateway through which the Oriental rug became Europeanized. That is to say, the original Oriental designs copied by the Spanish weavers gradually took on a purely European outlook over the years. Secondly because, for a reason still unknown, Spain introduced a completely different knotting technique from any other rug-producing country. Basically it is the Turkish knot which they use in Spain, but they tie it on one warp thread only, alternate warp threads being used, whereas the Turkish version is tied on two warp threads. The Spanish innovation makes for a rather loosely knotted fabric, but the wool content is almost the same as for Oriental carpets.

Although the earliest surviving examples of Spanish carpets are attributed to the fifteenth century, it is known that when Eleanor, the daughter of Ferdinand III of Castile, came to England to marry Edward I she brought carpets with her. Whether or not these were knotted, or even if they were of Spanish manufacture, is not known, but the records at least set a date when objects called carpets were already in use in Spain. There are still some fifteenth-century pieces to be seen in museums, all of which closely resemble the Turkish carpets of that era. Actually there are more fifteenth-century Spanish pieces preserved than any other type. Certainly by the end of the fifteenth century Spain was making carpets herself, even though the work may have been done by immigrants, as suggested by Van de Putt in 'Some 15th Century Spanish Carpets' (*Burlington Magazine* XIX September 1911). Although still showing Turkish treatment in the designs, the carpets also took on various Christian and heraldic devices, until the seventeenth century when what we regard as a Spanish design had evolved. Because of their background of centuries of Moorish domination, this transposition of design was easier in Spain than perhaps any other country in Europe. The main manufacturing places in the early days were Almeria and Alcaraz. Nowadays, Spain makes carpets of any size, design and colour, in either the Spanish knot or the true Turkish knot.

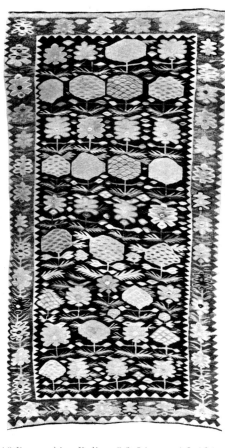

110 Bessarabian Kelim: 8 ft 9 ins × 4 ft 10 ins

# WHAT OF THE FUTURE?

111 Modern hand-knotted carpet reproducing an antique design

THE ORIENTAL RUG STORY can be told in a very few words — a period of surmise followed by some early authentic examples, after which there was a great awakening in both production and appreciation of the craft, leading up to the sixteenth and seventeenth centuries, and afterwards a slow decline until the nineteenth-century revival.

Unfortunately this revival came at a time when the inventive genius of man had led him to the substitution of mechanical aids and materials for the hand-operated utensils and natural materials always used hitherto. Instead of the wool being handspun, it could be done by machine. Lancashire could supply the cotton, and for dyestuffs the aniline dye was much easier to obtain then the berries, insects and other local products which had been used ever since textile weaving began. Change came gradually, of course, and in the matter of dyestuffs Persia at least rebelled against them, and forbade the use of them until the present century.

As time goes by, of course, there will be fewer and fewer pieces available for exhibition, and even for sale by way of trade, until eventually the only relics of the distant past will be in museums and large collections.

Fine old goods in mint condition have always been in short supply, but in the last twenty years, since the end of the Second World War, a somewhat greater demand for this type of merchandise, coupled with the fact that there are an old rug for this purpose, as the pile tufts are not long enough to re-tie, so the only way is to unravel old Kelims, and selvedges of rugs, where the yarn will be long enough to make knots. Unfortunately, old Kelims are also not found very often, so there are not many repairers today who are doing the real job of reparation. Eventually, however, all repairs will inevitably have to be done with new wool. What a pity — but all lovers of old rugs should feel obliged to take great care of them. Rugs deserve far more consideration than they normally receive. After all, two years of a man's life may be woven into the ordinary sized scatter rug, which is merely walked on and kicked about when it gets in the way.

Another reason for looking after rugs well is that in this way their investment value will be preserved. As a general rule, good rugs properly cared for will always sell well in the right market. It must be remembered, however, that the dealer has to make a profit on reselling it, so that the price he is prepared to pay will never reach the re-sale price. But a good Oriental rug which has given some years of use will not have lost much of its value over this period, always providing, of course, that it was bought at the right price in the first place.

fewer rugs available, has created a kind of famine never before experienced. The breaking up of large estates due to high estate duties has on occasions somewhat alleviated the position, but whereas in years gone by the large salerooms could offer every week many lots of good old pieces, today there is intense competition whenever a few pieces of the right class and condition appear. It was said above that a greater demand for Oriental rugs has been created in the recent past. This is true in certain countries due to the higher standards of living, to an awareness of the product not known previously. A great shortage is also evident in the producing countries themselves, although in some cases they are now in a position to buy them back on the world markets. Alas, in the United Kingdom at any rate, the progress is extremely slow. At this moment the total Oriental rug consumption within the country, and this includes mass-produced Indian carpets, consists of only approximately $2\%$ of the floor covering market.

112 Modern Turkish Saph

113 Old Saruk rug: 6 ft 11 ins × 4 ft 6 ins

There are still many great collections, the museums have a wealth of examples to show, and, incidentally, most of them can be visited without charge, but very few people seem to know anything whatever about these treasures. The glossy magazines expound on the subject of stately homes, but often a photograph of a room does not mention the rug or carpet. All the other items are fully described, but it appears that the floor is something to be avoided. It may be that this is good in the long run, because the carpet should be unobtrusive, like a good servant — not noticed in service, but sadly missed if absent. The future holds good prospects for the connoisseur. Many rugs being made today will undoubtedly stand the test of time but they must be chosen with care, and must be looked after properly. There are still some repairers of the old school but, as with most craftsmen, they are a dying race, and not many young ones are entering the craft. The art of repairing old rugs lies in the use of old wool for the new pile. It is not possible to use the pile of an old rug for this purpose, as the pile tufts are not long enough to re-tie, so the only way is to unravel old Kelims, and selvedges of rugs, where the yarn will be long enough to make knots. Unfortunately, old Kelims are also not found very often, so there are not many repairers today who are doing the real job of reparation. Eventually, however, all repairs will inevitably have to be done with new wool. What a pity — but all lovers of old rugs should feel obliged to take great care of them. Rugs deserve far more consideration than they normally receive. After all, two years of a man's life may be woven into the ordinary sized scatter rug, which is merely walked on and kicked about when it gets in the way.

Another reason for looking after rugs well is that in this way their investment value will be preserved. As a general rule, good rugs properly cared for will always sell well in the right market. It must be remembered, however, that the dealer has to make a profit on reselling it, so that the price he is prepared to pay will never reach the re-sale price. But a good Oriental rug which has given some years of use will not have lost much of its value over this period, always providing, of course, that it was bought at the right price in the first place.